Proven ways to build a healthy and happy family

Doc Pop's 52 Weeks of Active Parenting

by Michael H. Popkin, Ph.D.

Active Parenting Publishers
1955 Vaughn Rd., Suite 108
Kennesaw, GA 30144-7808
800-825-0060
770-429-0565
www.ActiveParenting.com

ISBN 1-880283-82-4
Library of Congress Control Number: 2004110649
Printed in Canada.
First edition.

NOTE: Every effort has been made to ensure that the information contained in this book is complete and accurate. However, neither the publisher nor the author is engaged in rendering professional advice or services to the individual reader. The ideas, procedures, and suggestions contained in this book are not intended as a substitute for consulting with a professional. Neither the author nor the publisher shall be liable or responsible for any loss or damage allegedly arising from any information or suggestion in this book.

Dedicated to Megan and Ben,
the most important children in the world
...to their mother and me.

Table of Contents

Introduction

About This Book . . .

Have you ever wondered why some families seem to thrive amidst the trials and tribulations of our hectic modern life while others thrash about bouncing from one problem to another in pain and frustration? No? Okay, how about this. Ever wonder how to get more joy and satisfaction out of family living while still imparting the character, values, and skills that will enable your kids to succeed in the world of the 21st century? Still no? How about *this* then. Ever wonder if aliens really built the pyramids, and if they did, did they leave any really good books on parenting behind? If so, I hate to tell you, but this is not that book.

This book was not left by aliens, nor, for that matter, was it handed down to me on Mount Sinai. It is simply the best of what I know about raising successful children and creating satisfying families. As such, it is a sort of "Doc Pop's Greatest Hits" of what has been found to be most effective by the millions of parents who have taken my parenting programs. (Not that they all wrote me, you understand. This is a bit of hyperbole, but still, I'll stand behind it.) I've been at this for some thirty years and I have yet to meet the parent who could not improve things at home at least a little with the help of some good information. This includes me, the humble parent of two outstanding teenagers. This book will help you, too. It may help you a little or it may help you a lot. That depends partly on you and how much you practice what I preach.

Which brings me to the question of why 52 weeks of Active Parenting? Why not 51 or 53? The reason is that there are exactly 52 lessons in parenting that you need to know in order to really cover all your bases. The fact that there are also 52 weeks in a year is merely a happy coincidence. I got lucky, that's all.

That last paragraph is nonsense, by the way. I chose 52 weeks so that you could take it slowly over an entire year and build your skills gradually while practicing new skills each week. Of course, you may prefer to proceed faster if you choose, but please be sure to practice the activities as you go, at least the ones that make sense to you. Because, as I like to say, it's not the information that's important, it's what you *do* with the information that's important. So give it a try each week, be patient, and then start noticing the positive changes.

Here's to your family: the most important family in the world!

"Doc Pop"

Michael H. Popkin, Ph.D.

The Purpose of Parenting

Every job worth doing well begins with an understanding of its purpose. Parenting, one of the most important and most challenging of all jobs, is no exception. So, what is our purpose as parents? To make sure the toys get picked up and the dog fed? To referee sibling battles and prevent food fights? To maintain enough sanity in our homes that the little men in white coats don't come calling? Sure, but it's also much more. Try this out:

The purpose of parenting is to protect and prepare our children to survive and thrive in the kind of society in which they will live.

In other words, parenting is about preparing our children for success in the fast-paced, high tech, multicultural, democratic society of the 21st century. That means instilling in them the skills and qualities that will enable them to thrive: qualities like courage, responsibility, mutual respect, cooperativeness; skills like problem solving, conflict management, empathy and communication. Whew! Makes you kind of tired just reading about it, doesn't it?

But what if the heavens parted and someone tapped you on the shoulder and whispered that you have been selected to rear the most important children in the world? How quickly would you feel energy pulse through your veins? And how seriously would you take that job? Would you get the training and support you need to do the job well? Would you give the job the time and attention it requires? Would you feel proud every day you got up and went to work? You bet! Well, guess what? You have been chosen to rear the most important children in the world—yours! Good luck.

Activity

Picture This!

Get a recent picture of each of your children. Paste or tape the picture in the areas marked below. Now stare at each picture. And as you are staring, think to yourself, *"This is the most important child in the world. And although every mother and father is also raising the most important child in the world, it is an awesome responsibility and one that I can proudly handle."* Next, write down three things that you like about each child in the space provided.

The most important children in the world:

Week 2

Every Day, A Little Play

Most parents are aware of how important discipline is to a child's development. Yet discipline does not occur in a vacuum. It occurs within the overall context of your relationship with your child. When that relationship is a good one, based on mutual respect and genuine caring, discipline is much easier and we have a greater influence on the decisions that our children make. But when the relationship is stressed and kids feel that the only time you even notice them is to say *"Stop!"* or *"Don't!"* then they often misbehave out of frustration and resentment.

To help build or maintain a positive relationship with your child, make sure you build time into each day to have fun together. It can be as brief as ten minutes of horseplay on a busy day or a whole afternoon together on a weekend. Better yet, why not rent a Lear jet for the week and take the whole family on a tour of favorite roller coaster parks with unlimited money for souvenir spending and all the ice cream the kids want three times a day? (Sorry, my twelve-year-old son inspired that one. Our fault though, we taught him to dream big.) The key is to make sure to choose an activity that you both enjoy. And it doesn't have to be expensive. Whether it is a board game, sport, an outing, rough-housing, cooking together, or destroying an entire army of terrorist invaders (I'm thinking video game here and not real life, but suit yourself), make sure this is a time free from discipline and confrontation. Make it a time to just enjoy yourselves and each other. You may be surprised how a little daily play can pay great dividends in so many other areas of your relationship with your child.

Activity

Taking Time for Fun

Take a minute to think about something fun that you have done with each of your children. Remember the good feelings that you had while doing this thing together. Try to picture the joy on your child's face while the two of you played together and how good she must have felt inside knowing that you valued her company so highly. Now plan to spend at least ten minutes every day this week doing something fun together and record your experiences below.

	What did you do, and how did it go?	How can you improve the experience next time?
Day 1		
Day 2		
Day 3		
Day 4		
Day 5		
Day 6		
Day 7		

Week 3

Problems Aren't All Bad!

Ever wonder what distinguishes healthy, happy families from those that flounder in endless frustration and turmoil, like in some TV shows? Well, it isn't the presence or absence of problems if that's what you're thinking. The fact is that all families have problems. The difference is that some families handle those problems effectively while others often resemble the Simpsons, blundering from one episode to another.

Another fact is that problems offer parents wonderful opportunities for teaching children qualities such as responsibility, cooperation, and courage, and skills such as conflict resolution, negotiation, and of course, problem solving. And since our purpose as parents as defined in Week 1 is to instill these and other qualities and skills that will enable our kids to survive in our modern democratic society, problems are truly opportunities for learning. Without them (and the motivation they provide), we might just sit around watching reruns of old sitcoms all day.

Notice and Appreciate the Bumps

A little boy was leading his younger brother up a mountain path to get a view from the top when the trail suddenly turned steep and bumpy. "How are we going to hike up this?" asked the little brother in dismay, "It's all covered with bumps." The big brother took his little brother's hand and calmly explained, "The bumps are what we walk on." True, the two brothers were never heard from again, but that's not the point. The point is that the bumps in life are our opportunities, so this week, find the problems that you want to work on in your family. And if your two kids take off hiking up a steep mountain without an adult, ground their little behinds for a month!

As you observe your family this week, write down some of the problems that you see as opportunities for teaching your children useful life lessons:

Problem	Qualities and Skills to be Taught
Example: Room is always messy	Value neatness and organization

Week 4

Defuse Power Struggles with The Method of Choice

I was visiting some friends who were in a mighty power struggle trying to get their five-year-old son to put on his coat so we could go out to dinner. After about fifteen minutes of pleading, whining, and threatening (and this was from the parents, not the child!) I called the father aside and asked him if his son had another coat. Fortunately he did, and I suggested that the father give his son a choice between the two coats. The father, who was willing to try anything short of child abuse at this point, gave his son the choice. The son, of course, chose the other coat, and we were out the door in thirty seconds.

Now, a lot of parents might be thinking, "Yeah, I'd give him a choice: a choice between putting on the coat or getting my hand across his behind!" And that would work, too. At least for a while, and then the child's resentment would build up and he is likely to resist you again about something else. The beauty of the Method of Choice is that it gives the child some legitimate power without him having to say "no" to get it!

Think about it: when you give your child an order instead of a choice, if he wants power then his only option is to refuse. By giving him an "either/or" choice *(Would you rather have orange juice or cranapple? Would you rather set your homework time before dinner or after?)* you give him power without him having to refuse you. It's a deceptively effective technique that not only sidesteps a lot of power struggles, but also prepares your child to make decisions. For older kids you can give more open-ended choices. *(What kind of juice would you like this morning? When would you like to schedule your homework time this semester?)* But for young kids, keep it simple with "either/or" choices.

Activity

Experimenting with Choices

Spend some time this week noticing when you give your child orders instead of choices. Then look for opportunities to provide choices that are within limits that are acceptable to you. For example, do not give your child the choice of eating his peas or leaving the table, and then when he chooses to leave the table, slap the table and yell, *"Sit back down and eat those peas!"* Only give choices that you can live with! And one other caveat, don't make *everything* a choice. Kids sometimes want and need clear directions from their parents. For example, as your four-year-old races for the street, it's not a good time to practice giving choices. It's a good time to yell, *"Stop!!!"* then run and grab him.

Being the creative parent you are, I'm sure you'll find plenty of safe and appropriate choices to experiment with. Jot down your results here.

Choice 1. _____

Result _____

_____

Choice 2. _____

Result _____

_____

Choice 3. _____

Result _____

_____

Week 5

When-Then Choices

Have you ever noticed how kids will often prefer to do what *they* want to do rather than what *we* want them to do? Good news, though: one of the simplest yet most powerful discipline methods for getting kids to do something that they resist doing is to use "when-then" choices. This technique is sometimes called "grandmother's rule," because by the time we have become grandparents most of us have figured this one out for ourselves anyway. It's a great method for avoiding power struggles while providing often needed motivation to children.

To use a "when-then" choice simply pair the thing that you want your child to do (for example, cleaning his room) with something that your child enjoys doing (like playing) so that the child must complete the first before being allowed to do the second. In other words, *"When you have cleaned your room, then you may play."* The implied choice is that if you chose not to clean your room, then you also choose not to play until you do.

As with all discipline, be willing to follow through with the consequences or the lesson will be lost. Make sure your voice is firm and calm, and make sure that the fun part is something that normally occurs. This is not a reward or bribe, but just an application of a sort of "work before play" family value. Some typical examples of "when-then choices" include:

- When you have brushed your teeth, then we will read your bedtime story.

- When you have done your homework, then you may play your video game.

- When pigs fly, then you may go to an R-rated movie.

When you have finished your meal, then you may have dessert. • When the two of you stop fighting, then I will continue driving.

Applying "Grandmother's Rule"

Write down a behavior that you want your child to do, but that she resists doing:

Next, write down an action or event that your child likes doing that might logically follow this behavior and that occurs regularly anyway:

Now, use the above to fill in the blanks:

When you have _____ ,

then you may _____ .

Try it the next time you have the opportunity and see how it goes. Remember, stay firm and friendly and be willing to follow through on the consequences. Also, if your child does do what you have asked, be sure to express your appreciation with encouragement.

Head Off Misbehavior *Before* It Occurs

Every child worth his video games knows that it is often easier to get forgiveness than permission. Hence, a lot of misbehavior results from us not being clear about our expectations beforehand. *"Oh, I didn't know you meant that I couldn't watch R-rated movies at someone else's house; I just thought you meant at our house."*

Sometimes this is legitimate, sometimes it's a smoke screen. But in either case, a lot of problems can be successfully headed off at the pass if we will take the time to sit down together and have a brief meeting about new situations and what is expected and agreed upon. This is not an opportunity for parents to just lay down the law. It's a chance for some "give and take" in negotiating clear agreements about what will and will not happen in a given situation.

Of course, parents as leaders in the family have the right and responsibility to limit behaviors that are unhealthy, unsafe, illegal, immoral, or violate family values. Still, that leaves a lot to discuss. The result is that everyone knows what's expected beforehand and kids feel empowered since they were part of the process.

Examples of events that might warrant a prevention talk include: spending the night out, going out for dinner together, going shopping, visiting grandma (*"Remember that Grandma doesn't really understand or appreciate bathroom humor."*), dating, going to a party, staying with a babysitter, having friends over, schoolwork, a family vacation.

Activity

Hold a Prevention Talk

Before your meeting, take a few minutes to write down as many concerns as you can think of as you anticipate potential problems. Then hold your meeting, "just to make sure we are all on the same page about _____." Keep your tone and attitude positive. You want to show confidence in your children's ability to make good decisions and behave appropriately for the situation. Some of the questions you might ask are:

"What kind of problems might come up that you would have to deal with?"

"How would you handle that?"

"What if...?"

Be sure to get agreements and stay encouraging. For example,

"Then we agree that..."

"And if _____ happens, then you will _____ and I will _____.

"Good thinking!" "I like that." "I want to make sure you have a good time, and that you stay safe and healthy."

Take notes from your meeting and afterward jot down agreements and expectations below.

_____

_____

_____

Mutual Respect

Respect is what you have to have in order to get. — Bernard Malamud

The audience sat with great anticipation as Oprah introduced a video clip from the new Active Parenting program that I had written and produced. As the expert guest I was more than a little anxious to see how the clip would be received. The scene opened as a mother and her five-year-old son sat on the sofa reading. Mother asks the son a question, but he is absorbed in his book and doesn't answer. She is upset by this and says, *"How many times do I have to ask you something? It is so rude of you to ignore me like that! When I ask you something I expect you to answer! Do you understand me, young man?!* The scene then plays again, but this time it is the son who asks the mother a question. She is absorbed in her book and fails to answer. He stands up, clearly upset, and says, *"Mother, it is so disrespectful for you to ignore me that way. How many times do I have to ask you a question? When I talk to you I expect you to listen! Do you understand me, middle-aged woman?!"* The clip ends as the audience howls with laughter, and I breath a sigh of relief. They got it.

Respect is so important for success in our diverse, democratic society that a lack of respect often breeds hostility and resentment. All parents want their kids to respect them, as well they should, but as the author Bernard Malamud once wrote, "Respect is what you have to have in order to get." In other words, the best way to teach our children respect is to show them respect. Yet as the video clip showed, we often talk to kids in ways that would be seen clearly as disrespectful if they talked that way to us. But if they do talk that way to us, it is good to be able to say, *"I don't talk that way to you and do not expect you to talk that way to me."* (And if they continue to talk to us disrespectfully, there are a number of discipline methods that we can use that we'll cover in later weeks.)

Remember When and Learn

Parents can learn a lot from remembering both the strengths and weaknesses of their own parents. Think back to your childhood and some of the ways your parents showed you respect or disrespect.

What are some ways your mother showed you respect?

What are some ways your mother was disrespectful to you?

What are some ways your father showed you respect?

What are some ways your father was disrespectful to you?

What are some ways you have been disrespectful to your children?

This week, to catch yourself before you behave disrespectfully to one of your children, imagine him as another adult. Speak and show the same respect that you would to another adult. Then answer the following:

What changes in your own behavior did you notice as a result of your attempts to be more respectful?

What changes did you notice in your child's attitude toward you?

Week 8

Take Care of the Caregiver

It takes a lot of energy to be an active parent. Imagine for a moment that your energy is contained in a pitcher of liquid (and if you are thinking "Yeah, a pitcher of margaritas," you need this chapter more than you realize). Throughout the day you are pouring out that energy—perhaps at work, with your partner, with friends, and of course with your children. At the end of a long day, that pitcher may be bone dry! Filling it back up is a matter of taking care of yourself—the caregiver. Parents who never think of themselves, their own needs and wants, often lack the emotional and physical energy to give their kids their best. Of course, some parents go too far the other way and spend too much time taking care of themselves, and as a result they ignore many of their children's legitimate needs and wants. As with most things, the key is in finding the right balance.

What can you do to refill your pitcher every day? Think about these four categories:

- **your health:** getting enough rest, nutrition, and exercise
- **your adult relationships:** talking with friends, making time for your partner if you are in a significant relationship, developing a close confidante
- **your mind:** finding healthy ways to relax, spending time outdoors, developing a hobby
- **getting organized:** making a "to do" list every day, keeping a calendar of what and when you have to do things, organizing each area of your home

Remember, a reasonable amount of self-care is not selfish. It's the way you re-energize yourself for your own well being and the well-being of your family. You can't be an effective parent for long without it!

Activity

Keep a Self-Care Chart

To help you focus on self-care this week, fill in the following chart with ideas for taking care of the caregiver. Get creative! Maybe a hot bath at night relaxes you for a good night's sleep. Maybe you've always wanted to sign up for an art class and now's the time. You might even be surprised how revitalizing cleaning out a cluttered closet can be. Experiment and find what's right for you—just keep the alcohol in moderation and no one-time quick fixes like a week in Hawaii! (Although regular adult vacations can certainly be part of your long-term plan!) Finally, put a check by each activity that you do this week, and then evaluate how you feel and what other results you notice.

Healthy body:

1. _____

2. _____

3. _____

Healthy mind:

1. _____

2. _____

3. _____

Relationships with others:

1. _____

2. _____

3. _____

Getting organized:

1. _____

2. _____

3. _____

Catch 'em Being Good

Let's do a quick one-question experiment. Are you aware of the temperature where you are right now? Chances are that unless you are either too hot or too cold you were not thinking about the temperature. We just rarely sit around thinking, "Gee, it sure is comfortable around here. I hope nobody messes with the thermostat or brings me a fluffy blanket." But let it get too hot or cold and see how our awareness levels shift. The same is true of our kids. As long as they are behaving well and doing what we would like we often fail to notice. But let them misbehave and see what happens to our awareness!

Although this selective attention works well with the temperature, it is a problem in parenting. As the famous psychiatrist Rudolf Dreikurs once said, *"Children need encouragement like plants need water."* This means that they need to hear from us about what they are doing well in order to grow into mentally healthy human beings.

"Good job, atta boy, atta girl, way to go, nice going, thanks a lot, that's the idea, I really like the way you…, I noticed how you…, keep it up, I'm proud of you!"

These encouragers build emotional muscle, positive behavior, and may even help develop intellectual functioning.

This week practice training yourself to notice all of the positive things that your children do, and comment on them in a supportive, affirming way.

Good job • Way to go • Nice going • Thanks a lot • That's the idea • Keep it up • I'm proud of you

Catch 'em Being Good (duh!)

Every day this week make a point to catch each of your children at least three times a day doing something positive. It can be as simple as their remembering to say "thank you," or as ambitious as working on improving their grades. The key is to be genuine in your encouragement as you let them know that you notice and appreciate their attitude and behavior. Use the chart below to record their positive actions and your encouraging words. Then notice how they respond during the week.

	Positive Behavior	Your Encouraging Response
Day 1		
Day 2		
Day 3		
Day 4		
Day 5		
Day 6		
Day 7		

How Well Do You Know Each Other?

Ever notice how an effective salesperson will get to know you a little bit before trying to sell you something? Salespeople know that you are more likely to buy from people you know and like. Parenting is similar, except that instead of selling merchandise, parents sell goals, attitudes, and behavior. A lot of parents will read the word "sell" and think I'm being too permissive. But how would you like it if a salesperson told you, *"You will buy this car because I'm the salesperson and I said so!"* I think you would find a new dealership. Winning kids over is a key to influencing them, and getting to know them better will help you do that. Plus, showing an interest in a person says that you care, and will usually open up communication. It also says that the other person is worth knowing better. Most people find that very encouraging.

Before asking your kids questions you may want to consult your dentist, because it can often feel like pulling teeth. A few non-dental tips may help:

- **Find a good time.** Dragging your kids away from their favorite video game so you can interview them is not going to win their cooperation. Bedtime is great because it means getting to stay up a little later.

- **Be encouraging,** or at least non-judgmental. If your kids read your mind and see a lot of negative thoughts about them and their answers you may as well kiss this interview goodbye.

- **Ask open-ended questions.** Asking "yes or no" questions will usually get a lot of "yes or no" answers. So, instead of asking, "Did you have a good day in school?" ("Yes.") try asking something more open-ended like, "What's something that happened in school today that surprised you?"

Find a good time • Be encouraging • Ask open-ended questions

Activity

Getting to Know You...

This interview activity will help you get a feel for how well you already know your child, while at the same time helping you get to know him better. First, fill in the interview with your best guesses at what he will answer. Then find a good time to ask him the same questions, writing down his answers so that later you can beat yourself over the head as you compare his answers with your guesses. Actually, take this in with a smile instead of a kick and you will both feel a lot better about the experience. If you have more than one child, interview each separately. And if you are like the lovely neighbors down the street from us with eight children, add the following question: *"What was I thinking?!"*

1. What is your favorite movie of all time and why?

2. What is your favorite TV show and why?

3. What is your favorite food of all time?

4. What is your favorite ice cream flavor?

5. If you could be a superstar, who would you be and why?

6. If you were given a million dollars to spend, what's the first thing you would spend it on? (After you buy your parents new cars, that is.)

7. If you had to pick one friend to spend a week with who would it be?

8. What is it about that person that you like?

9. What does that friend like about you?

10. What is one problem that you are working on solving?

Week 11

Who Owns the Problem?

In Week 3 we talked about how problems offer wonderful opportunities to teach children character, as well as skills for being successful. Now it's time to talk about solving those problems. The first step is to decide who has responsibility for handling a problem—you or your child. It's important to determine who owns the problem because what we do next depends on it. Parent-owned problems will be handled with *discipline* while child-owned problems will be handled with *communication/support skills*. Three hints will help you determine who owns the problem and who should be allowed responsibility for handling it:

1. With whose goals is the problem interfering?
2. Who is most bothered by the problem?
3. Is the problem a matter of health, safety or family values?

Consider these examples:

Problem...	Who Owns It?
Your child is making a lot of noise in a restaurant.	You do, because you (and other patrons) are bothered by her behavior.
Your child is upset because he didn't get invited to a birthday party.	You child does because it was his goal to be invited and he has the upset feelings.
Your child repeatedly fails to turn in his homework.	You do, because it is your goal to see that he completes school, leaves home, and doesn't mooch off you for the rest of his life.

On that last one, of course, your goal is to turn the problem over to your child, so you might consider this a "Shared" problem—which basically means you can't decide who owns the problem and will probably use a combination of discipline *and* support.

Activity

Determining Who Owns a Problem

First, practice recognizing who owns the problem with these three examples. (You can find the answers upside down on the back of your favorite breakfast cereal. If they aren't there, call the manufacturer and complain. And while you're at it ask why there is more sugar than honey in a cereal called "Honey Nut O's." Shouldn't they really be called "Sugar Nut O's? I think so.)

Problem...	Who Owns It, and Why?
Your child throws a baseball through the garage window.	
Your child got extra homework at school for passing notes.	
Your child keeps leaving his lights on in the bathroom in the morning.	

Next, write down three problems that occur at home this week, and then analyze who owns the problem. Try to find at least one problem owned by you and one owned by your child as we will use these to work on solutions in the weeks ahead.

Problem...	Who Owns It, and Why?

The answers to the three practice questions are "yours, your child's, and yours" in that order. (Pretend this is a cereal box.)

Week 12

Communication Blocks

The next four weeks are devoted to developing the communication skills needed to effectively help your child solve problems that she owns. However, before you can do this, you have to first make sure that when you open your mouth you aren't putting your foot into it. Read the definition of communication blocks to the left. In other words, you've blown it and your child clams up tighter than a CEO in front of a grand jury. Some communication blocks to be avoided are:

Commanding	"What you should do is…"
Giving advice	"Why don't you…"
Placating	"Everything will be okay, you'll see."
Interrogating	"What did you do to make him…"
Distracting	"Let's not worry about that, let's …"
Psychologizing	"Hmm…do you know why you said that?"
Being judgmental	"That wasn't a very smart thing to do."
Sarcasm	"Well, I guess that's just about the end of the world."
Moralizing	"You really should…"
Being a know-it-all	"I've seen this a hundred times and let me tell you…"

And these are just SOME of the ways we block communication. As one parent said, "I'm so good at communication blocks that I can use two or three of them at once!" The key is to identify our personal pitfalls and then be on guard against using them. Although our goal in using communication blocks is to help solve the problem, they often send the message that we don't respect our children's ability to deal with painful experiences and find useful solutions themselves. The result is that our kids shut us out and we lose a chance to be really helpful.

Catching Ourselves in the Blocks

Look at the list of communication blocks on page 30 and identify the three that you think you use most often. List them below. Then write what your intention is when you use them. And finally, what negative message you are sending your child that turns her off from sharing?

	My good intention	My negative message
Block **1:**		
Block **2:**		
Block **3:**		

Next, look for opportunities this week when talking with your child to catch yourself before you use these and other blocks. Write down the situation and the block you almost used (or did use) in the chart below. And if you were successful in avoiding the block, write down what you said instead.

Situation	Communication Block	What you said instead

Week 13

Listen Actively

I recall meeting a famous professional basketball player in the airport one time. As we stood there chatting about his career I noticed that his eyes kept darting around the concourse as if he were looking for other fans to talk to. His lack of focus and attention made me feel pretty small. (The fact that he was a good foot taller than me didn't help, but there's not much he could do about that.)

When our kids show us the trust to talk with us about a problem that they own (which, remember, means "own responsibility for solving"), the least we can do is give them our undivided attention and listen with our eyes as well as our ears. We've all known people who seem to listen to us completely when we share a concern or problem, just as we've all known people like my highly-paid basketball-dunking pituitary case in the airport. To listen actively to a child means **really thinking** about what she is saying and even "intuiting" the feelings and hidden messages behind the words. It means giving your full attention, keeping your own talk to a minimum, keeping the focus on her problem, and acknowledging what you are hearing. And this means asking clarifying questions, saying simple words of encouragement like "I see" or even "uh-huh," and summarizing what you hear them telling you. Of course, it also means avoiding communication blocks. (But you already know that, right?)

The result is that your child feels really listened to and cared about. This in itself is very encouraging and goes a long way toward helping your child solve problems. In the next few weeks we will take this a step further with a process called active communication to help your child become a successful problem solver.

What did you *really* do in school today?

We have all asked our kids, *"What did you do in school today?"* only to be told that age-old lie, *"Nothing."* Of course, what they really mean is either *"nothing significant to me"* or *"nothing that I want to talk to you about."* The activity for this week is to use active listening (while avoiding communication blocks) to really push through the resistance and engage your child in a brief conversation about what happened in school. If he is out of school on break or sick, then talk about whatever else he did today. You might begin by asking your child for some time. For example, *"May I have five minutes of your time?"* Or you might just find a convenient time when he is less likely to object, for example, while waiting to be served in a restaurant or at bedtime, when staying up a few minutes later is always an incentive. Be sure to be really interested in what he has to say and gently encourage him to share. For example, *"I really want to know. Tell me about social studies today…"*

After your talk, write down your answers to the following questions.

What did you like about how the talk went?

How did you handle your child's initial resistance, if you were successful?

What would you do differently next time?

Week 14

Respond to Feelings, Not Just Content

Listening actively to our kids is the first step in helping them learn to be problem solvers instead of blamers and excuse makers. The second step is to let them know that we care about them and their feelings. Why is this important? Because I'm the expert and I said so! Just kidding, but that kind of answer and parenting approach makes most kids feel about as cooperative as a rhino with a bad attitude. (Which is all rhinos from what I understand, which is why rhinos have never been domesticated, which, though interesting, is only pertinent to this book if you have a child who acts like a rhino, in which case see Week 4 on power struggles.) The real reason to care about your child's feelings is that you want him to care about what you think. That's how we influence kids. And as the saying goes, *"Kids don't care how much you know until they know how much you care."*

The catch is that you can't let your kids know how much you care by just telling them, "I care." You have to show them. One way to do that is by listening for their feelings and not just the content of what happened. When you can identify a feeling and relate it back to your child, you let her know that how she feels really does matter. *(You sound like you are really angry. I can see how hurt you were. That was really frustrating, wasn't it?)* When we respond to a child's feelings and get it right, an amazing thing happens. She nods her head and continues to share. When we miss, she has a perfect opportunity to correct us. Either way, the communication is enhanced. Plus, by naming feelings for children, we are encouraging them to express themselves through words instead of acting out their negative feelings with misbehavior.

That was really frustrating, wasn't it? • I can see how hurt you were. • You sound like you're really angry.

Reporters Need Not Apply

Good reporters know the importance of asking the "W" questions: who, what, where, when, and why. That's great, but what we need right now are parents to ask themselves the "how" question. As in, *"How is my child feeling about that?"* So, if you happen to be a Pulitzer Prize-winning reporter this is going to be a very tough activity. It's okay to ask the "W" questions, but when you respond, I want your response to include a word that describes what you think your child is feeling. (Even better would be what you *feel* your child is feeling, but I won't quibble.)

Do not engage your child in a lengthy conversation. Wait until we cover the next couple of weeks before you do that. Instead, just look for opportunities this week to identify what your child is feeling and reflect it back. Use a tentative form. For example, *"It sounds like you felt…"* or *"I guess you were…"* This way your child can easily correct you when you miss, as we all do.

Jot down some of the feeling words and phrases that you used and how your child seemed to respond to your expressions.

Feeling word	What you said	How child responded
_____	_____	_____
_____	_____	_____
_____	_____	_____

Look at Alternatives and
Evaluate Consequences

Continuing with the active communication process that we have been working on (and by "we" I mean "you"), let's assume your child has a problem, you
have taken the time to listen actively, and you are responding to his feelings as
well as to the content of what he is saying. This may be enough support to help
him reach a good decision on his own. But maybe not. A lot of times kids will gain
some clarity about a problem and their feelings about that problem, but then run
off to solve the problem with a half-baked plan that only makes it worse. Our job as
parents is to help our kids slow down and think about the consequences of possible solutions before they take action. This way they run off whole-baked which
is much more promising. Asking questions like the following can help:

- What *do* you *think* will happen if you try that?
- What *else* could you try?
- What *do* you think you can do to improve things?
- Have you thought about changing your name and moving to Timbuktu?

Keep in mind that your child owns the problem, so this is not an attempt
to tell him how to *solve* his problem. Rather, it is an attempt to help him
understand his choices and begin learning to predict the consequences of
those choices. This is not a perfect science, and there will be times when
the consequences do not work out like either of you thought. When that
happens (and you should always follow up on a talk by asking your child
how it did work out) go back to the three active communication steps
that we have been talking about: listen actively, respond to feelings, and
help your child look at new alternatives and evaluate the possible consequences.

What do you think you can do to improve things? • What do you try? • What else could you try? • What do you think will happen if you try that?

Activity

Palms Up

Parenting often drives people to say "bottoms up" as they look for relief by altering their state of consciousness. I prefer you think "palms up," which is a physical action of turning both palms up towards your child in a symbolic gesture that says, *"The decision is in your hands, not mine."* This palms-up gesture and attitude reassures the child that you are here to help and not to take over. That buys you influence. Of course, if it is an empty gesture and you *do* try to take over, then you'll find your child doing that clam impersonation we talked about earlier.

Find a time this week to talk with your child about a problem that she owns. Listen actively and respond to feelings. Then at some point look at your child gently and turn your palms up while saying something like, *"I don't know what your decision will be, but I would like to help you think about your choices. What do you think you might do?"* (Or if they have already told you something they might do, you could ask, *"What do you think will happen if you try that?"*) Afterwards, evaluate the process below.

What did you like about how the conversation went?

How did your child seem to respond to the palms up message?

What will you do differently next time?

Week 16

Bedtime Routines

Show me a child who wants to go to bed on time and I'll show you a child who is having much too good a time in dreamland. The natural course of events is for parents to tell kids to go to bed and for kids to ignore them. This usually goes on until the parent gets angry and threatens to punish before the child eventually slouches towards his room to be nagged some more. And yet, there is another way.

The key to bedtime is to establish a routine. A good routine with young children starts with bath time. You can make this fun by including some peppy music and favorite toys. Next comes flossing and brushing. (*"Can you open your mouth wide like a lion? Wow, I think I see an antelope down there!"*) And then, the highlight of the evening—reading time. This is a great way to wind down while also helping your child academically. With older kids and teens, you might substitute some quiet talk time. Next, it's lights out, prayers if you so desire, a special poem or saying, and perhaps a regular ritual like back scratching. And finally, don't forget the three words that every child longs to hear every day: "Here's the remote." I mean, *"I love you."*

The idea is to create a chain of events that mixes pleasant activities with "the little death" of having to go to sleep. Then, if your child balks at one of the links in the chain, say taking a bath, all you have to say is, *"Okay, honey, if you don't want to take a bath then hop right into bed and I'll turn off the lights."* In other words, if your child breaks the chain then it's straight to bed and she misses out on other fun parts of the chain. Stay firm and friendly and your child will soon adjust to the routine and go to bed happily ever after. (At least most of the time, anyway.)

Setting Up a Bedtime Routine

Think about how you can create a routine that incorporates some fun and some tenderness into the end of every day. Jot down what you are doing or plan to do in the space below, and then evaluate and modify as you try it with your child or children. And if you are stuck, don't hesitate to ask your child for some ideas.

Bedtime Routine Chart

Sample List	Your List	How did it go?	What will you change?
Bath time with music and toys and play			
Brush and floss teeth			
Story time–reading to your child			
Lights out			
Prayers			
Poem			
Back scratch			
"I love you."			

Say "I Love You" Every Day

Ten out of ten cardiologists agree: the heart is a very important organ. Without it, life just wouldn't be the same. Of course, they're just talking about the physical stuff—arteries, ventricles, blood flow, chambers of secrets, and those basic keep-you-alive sorts of things. When *I* talk heart, I'm talking about the really important stuff: courage, persistence, love. This is the stuff that makes a heartbeat worth having.

When the star pitcher for the Pittsburgh Pirates, Tim Wakefield, was once asked before his first postseason start if he was nervous, he replied, "No, because whatever happens tonight, I know that tomorrow three things will still be true: my parents will still love me, my friends will still love me, and God will still love me." Feeling loved is vital to our well-being, sense of self-esteem, and the very courage it takes to face life's challenges.

Some parents find it difficult to express the love they feel for their children in words. They prefer to show their affection with actions: a hug, a pat, or an endearing gesture. If you are one of these parents, get over it! Nonverbal communication is great, but your kids also need to hear the words *"I love you"* every day and twice on Sunday (just to start the week off right). Some parents find it difficult to even feel love for their children when misbehavior, anger, and rebellion characterize the relationship. To these parents I say, and you may have heard this before, get over it! Down deep in your heart you love your kids in spite of the conflicts, and the sooner you rediscover this love and express it, the sooner those conflicts will begin to resolve. (If you need a little help, go rent the movie *Pieces of April*. It's a small gem that packs a big message on the subject at hand.)

Three Creative Ways to Say "I Love You"

Often, saying "I love you" (and for this exercise I'm talking about saying it to your kids, not looking at yourself in the mirror and saying it to that stylish hunk or dish staring back at you) becomes a rote habit. Something we automatically say at bedtime or as they leave for school or juvenile court in the morning. This isn't all bad, though, especially if you get an "I love you, too" (often expressed by busy children as "loveyoutoo") in return. So, don't stop these good habits, but rather supplement them with three creative ways to say "I love you." Some ideas:

- Write a short poem and leave it someplace unexpected where they are sure to find it—like on the video game screen:
  Roses are red, your fingers are blue, from playing so long, but I love you!
- Play knock-knock: *"Knock knock." "Who's there?" "I-luv." "I-luv who?" "I love you!"*
- Sneak up on them and put your hands over their eyes:
  "Guess who?" "Daddy!" "Yes, and I love you!"
- Tell them profoundly:
  "I want to tell you something really important." "What?" "I really, really love you."

You can either come up with your own creative ways or borrow mine. The key is to give them a little unexpected jolt so they are tuned in, and then take aim at their heart. Afterwards, jot down what you did and how it went.

What you did and said	How your child responded
1.	
2.	
3.	

Week 18

Family Meeting: No Smoking

There are two reasons for this week's topic: one, family meetings are good, and two, smoking is bad. Let's say it together, *"Family meetings: good. Smoking: bad."* So, if you smoke yourself—which is an interesting image, rolling yourself up into a cigarette and then smoking it—the next time you have a craving to light up, why not have a family meeting instead? (That's a little joke between me and you. I know that smoking is tough to quit, which is why you need to work extra hard to make sure that your children don't ever start.)

When holding a family meeting on any topic make sure that you don't turn it into a lecture. This should be an open discussion in which you ask good questions to generate dialog, then use your active communication skills to listen to your children's answers and help them think it through. Finally, respectfully give your own good reasons for not wanting them to smoke. There are plenty of sources of good information about why smoking is a bad idea. My favorites are the website www.KeepKidsFromSmoking.com and a chapter on talking to kids about not smoking in the book *Getting Through To Your Kids*. (And since I wrote both they are likely to remain my favorites for some time.)

Besides the health risks involved in smoking be sure to talk about the more immediate effects of smoking—like smelly breath, yellow teeth, skin that ages too fast, and the fact that it is illegal for children and teens. Make sure your kids also know that it is against your family rules for them to smoke and that you would be upset with them if they did. Finally, find some good visuals of the negative side of smoking. There are lots of print ad campaigns against teen smoking that you can cut out or find on the Internet. Visuals give your arguments some real "yuck" effect.

Hold a Family Meeting

To help you plan for this family meeting, fill in the chart below with some of what you plan to say. You can always *ad lib* as you get into the meeting, but it helps to have done some planning first.

Examples	What You Plan to Say
1. Kick off "I called this meeting to talk about a very important topic, one that might save your life one day. That topic is smoking."	
2. Questions to generate discussion: "While you are moaning and groaning about this topic, how about taking a look at this picture of what a smoker looks like after he's been at it awhile. How would you like to end up looking like that?" "What are some reasons you think smoking is a really bad idea?" "How do you feel when you see teens smoking?"	
3. Points to make: • Smoking kills and/or reduces quality of life (cough cough) • Makes you look and smell yucky • Makes your skin age about twice as fast • Is illegal for teens • Is against our family's rules • Will mean we have to keep a closer eye on you if you do smoke—for example, fewer parties, etc. • We love you and care about you and want you to grow up healthy and strong	

Understand Your Child's Goal
When He Misbehaves

News flash: *Kids don't do what doesn't work.* If your kids are misbehaving repeatedly there must be something they are getting out of it: their "payoff." And guess who is usually the one doing the paying off? Probably you. People, including kids, are less motivated by causes in their past than they are by goals in their future. So, if you can figure out what they want ("goals") then you have a better chance of not paying them off. It may help to know that there are five main goals, and how kids approach these goals can be through positive behavior or through misbehavior. Our job is to avoid paying off their misbehavior and redirect them toward positive approaches to their goals. The following list may help:

BELONGING <u>Negative approach</u>: undue attention-seeking. <u>Parent's payoff</u>: nagging, reminding, lecturing. <u>Instead</u>: act more, talk less, and use logical consequences.

POWER <u>Negative approach</u>: rebellion. <u>Parent's payoff</u>: fighting or giving in. <u>Instead</u>: Withdraw from the power struggle, talk about it after cooling off, and use the FLAC Method (which we'll cover in Week 24).

PROTECTION <u>Negative approach</u>: revenge. <u>Parent's payoff</u>: Punish more severely, which justifies their desire to get even. <u>Instead</u>: avoid temptation to hurt them back, find out what's hurting them, use the FLAC Method.

WITHDRAWAL <u>Negative approach</u>: avoidance. <u>Parent's payoff</u>: Give up on them. <u>Instead</u>: stay encouraging, break it down to baby steps, get help if you need it.

ADVENTURE (teen years) <u>Negative approach</u>: reckless thrill seeking. <u>Parent's payoff</u>: Ignore or punish too severely. <u>Instead</u>: redirect toward positive adventures, use respectful forms of discipline.

Identifying Your Payoffs

Start thinking in terms of your child's goals and see if you can avoid paying off those goals when she misbehaves. We will be covering more discipline tools that you can use in the weeks ahead, so don't worry too much about what to do instead. Right now, just focus on noticing the role *you* play in paying off the misbehavior. Use the chart below to help you identify your child's goal and negative approach.

If you FEEL...	and your child's RESPONSE to correction is to...	then his negative approach and goal is probably...	How did you pay off (or avoid paying off) your child's approach?
Annoyed	stop the misbehavior, but resume it again pretty soon	undue attention seeking for the goal of belonging.	
Angry	resist you or give in to fight again later	rebellion for the goal of power	
Hurt	hurt you more or escalate the behavior	revenge for the goal of protection	
Hopeless	become passive, refuse to try, give up	avoidance for the goal of withdrawal	
Unusually afraid	take even more risks	reckless thrill seeking for the goal of adventure	

Week 20

Polite Requests

We are going to begin looking at some discipline skills for redirecting our children's misbehavior during the next few chapters. But first, have you ever been asked or told to do something in such a rude or offensive way that even though you really didn't mind doing it you did mind the way in which it was demanded—so much that you either openly refused or at least sabotaged your own efforts by complying in a way that failed to please the #%$* anyway? If you answered "no," I can recommend some good books on repressed memory retrieval.

The fact is that we often speak to children in such a disrespectful way that we set ourselves up for a power struggle before we even get going. Life in our democratic society means that we are all entitled to be treated respectfully, even when we are being disciplined by an authority. Woe to the boss who thinks he can get away with berating an employee unmercifully or a police officer who thinks he can lambaste a speeder with expletives while writing out a ticket.

Remember the video scene mentioned in Week 7 when a mother asks her child a question while he is engrossed in his reading? When he fails to answer she chastises him soundly. If you had trouble recognizing mother's behavior as disrespectful, remember the next scene when the tables are turned and the son stands up and shouts, *"Mother! Why do I have to repeat myself?! When I talk to you I expect you to listen! It is so disrespectful for you to ignore me like that! Do you understand me, middle-aged woman?!"*

There is no doubt that if we allowed our children to talk to us the way we often talk to them that we'd be in real trouble. But that's the subject of a future chapter. For now, let's work on talking to our kids in the way we would like them to talk to us.

Three Polite Requests

Rather than focusing on times you might talk to your kids disrespectfully I want you to make a conscious effort to ask them very politely (not mealy-mouthed syrup-dripping nauseatingly condescendingly sweet polite, but rather firm, clear, and respectfully polite) to change a behavior. For example,

> Steven, would you please make a point of putting your dirty dishes in the dishwasher after you've had a snack?

> Jessy, please be sure to turn off the lights in your bathroom when you come to breakfast in the morning. That will help us save electricity.

> Son, I don't talk to you that way and I don't expect you to talk to me that way. Do you understand me?

Then, because I live to make clever little charts for you to fill out, please use the following to record your heart-warming successes. And by success, I don't necessarily mean that your child will change her behavior (you should be so lucky!) but rather your success at laying the moral groundwork for demanding that your child treat you respectfully also. We will cover some other discipline skills in the coming weeks that you can use if the misbehavior continues.

Behavior you want to change	Your polite request	Child's response

Week 21

If a Polite Request Doesn't Work, Try an "I" Message

As I said last week, polite requests will not always work to change a misbehavior, either because the child is getting some kind of pay-off from the misbehavior and wants to continue getting it or the misbehavior has become a bad habit and it's hard to break bad habits, which is bad. (But it's also hard to break good habits, which is good.) The upshot is that you often need firmer discipline tools. The key is to get progressively firmer until you get results. Overkill is just bad parenting, and it doesn't teach character, only fear (of you!). And that isn't good for you, your child, *or* the relationship. So, when using discipline it is always best to proceed gently and in small increments until you get the results that you want.

A good, clear, firm communication skill for changing misbehavior is the *"I" message.* The "I" is in sharp contrast with the "you" messages that most parents use to change behavior. Always saying "you" tends to be a harsh, blaming sort of communication that often goes like this: *"You never..." "You always..." "Why do you..." "You make me so mad!"* This usually backfires. The "I" message is constructed in four parts. For example, let's say your child tends to speak to you disrespectfully, and your polite request just didn't cut it. So, you sit him down and say...

> **I have a problem with...** you using that sarcastic tone of voice when talking to me.
> **I feel...** angry when I hear it,
> **Because...** it's disrespectful and I don't talk to you that way.
> **I would like for you to...** talk to me respectfully.

"I" messages won't solve all problems, but you will be surprised how often they do work.

· 48 ·

Activity

Construct Two "I" Messages and Call Me in the Morning

I'm only kidding about the call me part, but I'm very serious about the construction job. (Try to keep that straight as I'm a late sleeper and don't really want to talk to you anyway. This is a book. I wish you well, but I'm not your new best friend. Stop crying, I'm only kidding. You can call me any time. Here's my number: 202-456-1414. Just ask for the President.)

Think of two problem behaviors that you would like to change in one or more of your children (or spouse for that matter—this stuff works with anyone). Write them down in the space provided and construct an "I" message for each. Use at least one of them during the week and write down your results. Again, if the results are not what you want, keep reading...we have firmer methods ahead.

"I" Message #1:

I have a problem with _____ .

I feel _____ ,

because _____ .

I would like _____ .

"I" Message #2:

I have a problem with _____ .

I feel _____ ,

because _____ .

I would like _____ .

Firm Reminders: The "KISS" Rule
(Keep It Short and Simple)

When kids don't do what you ask them to do, even when you have used a polite request *and* an "I" message, sometimes a "firm reminder" is called for. This is a stronger communication that sounds a little bossy, but, hey, it's called for since they keep ignoring us and we aren't about to blow our cool with a lot of screaming and yelling which gives them a big fat payoff in the power goal department. *("Look how powerful I am: I got him to blow his stack by just ignoring him!")* The idea behind a firm reminder is to tell them in as few words as possible what you want them to do. And by "as few words as possible," I mean ignore all the rules of grammar and syntax that you so diligently learned from that mean old English teacher years ago and get right to the meat and potatoes of the communication. By using a firm tone of voice and keeping it short and simple you get through to them before they have a chance to tune out. (This is the problem with mini lectures. We go on and on until they have a chance to adjust to our outrage and tune us out again. Just KISS them and they will hear you much better.) For example:

The Problem: Your child is beginning to yell at you.
Firm Reminder: "Caryn, lower your voice, now."

The Problem: Your child has ignored your request to make his bed and is playing a video game.
Firm Reminder: Turn off the TV and say, "T.J...bed...now."

The Problem: Your child is supposed to be taking a bath but instead is continuing to design a nuclear powered personal flight machine.
Firm Reminder: "Albert...bath...now." (Well, even geniuses need good hygiene.)

Activity

KISS Them with Firm Directions

This week's activity is to practice keeping it short and simple when your child does not respond to your polite requests or "I" messages. Remember to resist the temptation to lecture them on their thoughtlessness and how much you do for them and why can't they just show a little consideration and act more responsibly like their sister. Such lectures, even with less criticizing, usually backfire in the long run by either producing a childhood disease called "parent deafness" or else triggering their revenge gene into action later.

Look for opportunities to practice the KISS rule and then fill in the blanks in the chart below.

Child's misbehavior	Your firm reminder (KISS)	Child's response

Chances are that your child will respond to a good firm reminder. However, if they continue to "forget" the next time and you have to continue to remind them, then some firmer discipline is needed (and we're getting there next week). After all, at some point they need to remember on their own (unless your secret goal is to make sure they continue to need you for the rest of their natural lives, in which case be sure to do the opposite of everything I suggest in this book and there'll be a good chance they'll never leave home.)

Logical Consequences vs. Punishment

Here's my favorite cartoon of all time by the late great cartoonist/child "psychologist," Hank Ketchum. Dennis the Menace is coloring on the walls when his mother walks in and says, "How many times have I told you not to draw on the walls? Go sit in the corner and think about what you have done." "Aw, mom, that's kid stuff," says Dennis. "Well," says his mother, "How should I punish you instead—no TV for a week?" "Naw, that never works," says Dennis. "How about a spanking?" replies his mother. "I'm way too big for a spanking," retorts Dennis. "I've got just the thing," says mother, who leaves the room returning a minute later with a pail of water and a sponge. "Wash it all off," she says, "and no slopping the water around." Dennis, hard at work washing the wall, says to himself, "Boy, this stuff sure goes on a lot easier than it comes off!" The punch line occurs when mom returns to see the wall only half cleaned and does not see Dennis anywhere. "Dennis?" she calls. "Right here in the corner," he calls from his rocker, "thinking about what I have done!"

Humor aside, the beauty of this cartoon is that mother has stumbled on a first-rate discipline method called "logical consequences." The difference between logical consequences and punishment is that they are logically connected to the misbehavior rather than arbitrary. After all, what does sitting in the corner have to do with coloring on the walls? When we connect the consequence logically to the misbehavior, kids not only are more likely to see the justice in *our* actions, but they learn to be responsible for the consequences of *their* actions.

Activity

Use a Logical Consequence Instead

Look for opportunities this week to get out of the punishment rut, and instead use a logical consequence to help redirect your child's misbehavior. If your firm reminders (KISS) method isn't working, this is a good problem for a logical consequence. Or, you can look for other problems for this activity. Just follow these guidelines, and as always, then fill in the ever-present chart below.

1. Give a choice. "Dennis, in the future either color on paper or I will take away the crayons for a week."
2. Keep your tone of voice firm and calm. (No anger or yelling.)
3. Make sure you are willing and able to enforce the consequences.
4. Expect testing. Remember, your child is used to getting a payoff for his misbehavior, so expect him to test you to see if you will really follow through consistently. This means that you may have to use the consequence several times before it really works.

Problem Behavior	Logical consequence (Expressed as a choice)	Child's response	What you will do (if anything) next time

FLAC: The Ultimate Discipline Method

If you are thinking, "Oh, boy, here's where this joker finally gives us something to put the fear of God into that disobedient brat of mine," you are likely to be a little disappointed in the FLAC method. But if you recognize by now that what we are after is building character and not blind obedience then you will be quick to see the brilliance (if I do say so myself) of the FLAC method. We have covered each part of FLAC in previous weeks, but now we can put them all together.

F...eelings. As I mentioned in Week 14, kids need to know that we care about their feelings before they care about how much we know (or in this case, what we want). Acknowledging feelings can also help sidestep a power struggle.

L...imits. Remind them of the limits of the situation. "Because I said so" is an invitation to a power struggle, so try "because this is what is necessary for the situation." This means it's a matter of health, safety or family values.

A...lternative. Nobody likes to hear "no" for an answer, and though it's part of our job to set and enforce limits as parents, we can soften the "no" with an alternative that is acceptable to both us and our child. In Week 4, I talked about the power of choices. This is a good time to use them.

C...onsequences. Often the first three steps of FLAC are enough to gain your child's cooperation and avoid a power struggle. However, if the child continues to misbehave a logical consequence is called for.

Remember that the goal is to neither fight nor give in. You are not the enemy, you are an ally working with your child to find a solution that is acceptable to you both. When that isn't possible, you are still the parent who must enforce the reasonable limits of the situation.

Use FLAC to Reduce the FLACK

Look for an opportunity or two to use the FLAC method with one of your children this week. Then fill in the blanks and evaluate the experience.

F...Acknowledge your child's FEELINGS

"I can hear how much you'd like to stay up late and watch that television show tonight..."

_____

_____

L...State the LIMITS of the situation

"...but you need to get nine hours of sleep so you will be rested for school tomorrow, stay healthy and keep growing."

_____

_____

A...Look for an ALTERNATIVE

"I tell you what. How about if I record it for you and you can watch it tomorrow?"

_____

_____

C...If necessary use a LOGICAL CONSEQUENCE

"I really understand that you want to stay up late tonight and watch it, but I don't want you to be tired tomorrow. So, you can either go to bed right now and I will record it for you or you can keep arguing with me and miss it altogether. It's your choice."

_____

_____

How did it go? What will you do differently next time?

_____

_____

_____

Week 25

Use a Positive "I" Message to Encourage Positive Behavior

We've been focusing on how to redirect our kids' behavior from negative to positive ways of reaching their goals. I hope by now that you are seeing positive changes in their behavior. If you aren't, you probably aren't even reading this, having become discouraged, disheartened, and in an "I-give-up-this-guy-stinks" funk. All of which conveniently brings us to the subject of discouragement. When people of any age become discouraged, their behavior becomes less productive or even downright negative, and they may give up altogether. (This happened to me on a recent home plumbing project, but that's for another book, *My Life As An Unhandyman*, soon to be published by my plumber's trade association.)

One sure way for you to discourage your kids is to ignore their positive efforts to improve. Their perspective becomes "Why bother? They never notice when I do." The key to the powerful tool of encouragement is to train ourselves to notice *and comment on* their positive efforts as well as improved behavior. I talked about this in Week 9 under the topic "Catch 'em being good" and I haven't changed my mind about that chapter yet. More recently in Week 21, I covered a communication method called an "I" message. This was a method of confronting a child about a misbehavior. The flip side of an "I" message is something I call a *positive "I" message* (clever, huh?) and it also has four parts:

1. **Tell them what you like...**
2. **Say how you feel...**
3. **Tell them why..**
4. **Offer to do something for your child.** Keep it simple. Keep it logical and more like a celebration and win/win than a reward.

Catch 'em Doing Good with a Positive "I" Message

Since positive "I" messages are a little more complicated than a simple word of encouragement, try writing your message in the space below before you deliver it to your child. Make sure that it is for something that she is making a genuine effort to improve and that you are not just blowing smoke. Once you are satisfied with your words, find an opportunity to tell her how you feel face to face. Then evaluate the experience in the space provided. (If you are still having trouble with this, just be glad I haven't asked you to repair a leaky toilet!) Here's an example to get you started:

"I like the way you are remembering to turn off the lights in the bathroom in the morning. I feel good knowing that you heard my concerns about wasting electricity, because in our family we try to conserve energy and other resources. How about if we use some of the money we are saving on electricity to rent a video we can all watch together this weekend?"

What's the behavior your child is working to improve?

"I like _____ .

I feel _____ ,

because _____ .

How about if we_____?"

How did your child respond?

_____

_____

Your Temper:
Use It, Don't Lose It

Anger is a wonderful emotion. It tells us that something is not going well and that we need to get up off our behinds and do something to change it. The trouble is that most people ignore their anger when it first rumbles. In fact, think of yourself as having a thermometer with a bulb of red liquid in the bottom running from your stomach, up through your esophagus, and out your mouth. The first signs of anger are the bubbling of that red liquid in the bulb at the bottom in your stomach. As you ignore this bubbling anger the problem just gets worse and the message gets louder until it eventually spurts up the tube and out of your mouth in a hostile and obnoxious rage. This angry outburst is a primitive bullying tactic designed to give you the energy to act *and* to intimidate the other person (in this case your child) into doing what you want him to do. It sometimes works in the short run, but usually leads to more rebellious or revengeful behavior in the long run.

Instead of using your anger primitively, you can use it to take positive disciplinary action. It will help that you have been learning some new methods of influencing your child. It may also help to remember that when you lose your temper you have lost the power struggle, because to a child it looks like they are controlling your emotions—which is pretty powerful. Instead, take action when you are still in that "firm" frame of mind and tone of voice, and your anger will be at just the right level—the level that says, *"I'm not your enemy, but I do mean business."*

The Bathroom Technique

The more your child glares at you, the angrier you get. The more you act angry, the more defiant she gets. The more she digs her heels in, the more you feel you're going to blow your top!

Sound familiar? This is a classic power struggle. The way out is to remove yourself from the fight. The renowned psychiatrist Rudolf Dreikurs had an almost foolproof method. Just take a deep breath and say these magic words: *"I'm going to the bathroom."* Then walk to the nearest bathroom and stay there until you both calm down. You might keep a copy of this book in there, too, so that you can reread the sections on discipline and figure out how to use your temper constructively when you come out. The great thing about the bathroom is it's the one place in the house where people are usually allowed some privacy. So, lock the door and take a few deep breaths.

Of course, the exception is if you have a young child who might hurt himself while you're gone. In that case, you can say, *"I think we both need a time out. Let's send ourselves to our rooms for a little while."* This still breaks the power struggle, and also it adds a little unexpected humor that can also shift the emotional gears.

After you've tried the bathroom technique, fill in the blanks below...and don't forget to wash your hands.

What was the power struggle about? _____

How did you use the bathroom technique? _____

How did your child respond? _____

What will you do differently next time? _____

Handle Temper Tantrums with Grace

Parents, as we all know, aren't the only ones in the family to sometimes blow their stack and mishandle anger. Kids have also been known to throw a wide variety of tantrums either out of frustration or to just get their own way. In this era of zero tolerance for violence in school, the wise parent (and even the wiseguy parent who doesn't want his child to get expelled from preschool) will take the time to teach his child how to manage his temper. A few basic family rules enforced with some consistent logical consequences are a good start. For example:

Rule: People aren't for hitting.
Logical Consequence: Either play without hitting or play alone in your room. (Of course, parents can't hit either, which means no spanking.)

Rule: You break it, you buy it."
Logical Consequence: Either hit something unbreakable when you want to hit something (like a box or a pillow) or use your allowance to replace what you damage.

Rule: Keep your anger respectful.
Logical Consequence: Either talk respectfully about what you want or you don't even get a chance to get it. (No cussing, cursing or disrespectful tone from kids means that we have to do the same toward them.)

Rule: When in doubt, call time out.
Logical Consequence: When either parent or child feels herself about to break a rule, take a time out. (Separation is often the key to defusing an angry confrontation.)

Get Something Cold to Drink
and Put Up Your Feet

Let's face it. If you are dealing with tantrums you're probably exhausted and need a break. Go back and reread Week 8, "Take Care of the Caregiver," and make sure that you do whatever helps you to refill your pitcher of energy. And I won't even ask you to fill in one of my priceless charts this week. Now go on, stop blithering, and get that cold drink.

After your time out, these tips will help your child handle anger more constructively:

- Talk to her about the problem and the need to learn to handle anger well. Acknowledge that anger is a natural and okay emotion, but explain rules that apply.

- Agree on some ways to express anger appropriately: telling you she is angry, hitting a special punching bag or a pillow.

- When a child is out of control, try the following to see what works :

  – Talk to him calmly. Ask him to take deep breaths.

  – With younger kids, try putting your arms gently around him and telling him it's going to be okay. (Sometimes this is necessary to restrain an out-of-control child; sometimes it is just a means of providing the soothing quality of body contact. With very active kids beware of the painful head-butt. I still have scars to prove its danger.)

  – Ask him a question that requires some thinking. An emotional outburst short circuits the thinking brain. If you can get him thinking again, it will disengage the emotional outburst. Sometimes humor can do the same thing.

If none of these methods work, call Grace. She's a child neuropsychiatrist who can see if your child has a serious problem that needs intervention. (Kidding about the name, but not about the evaluation. Some hyper-angry kids do have a real problem that needs professional intervention. So, go check it out…with Grace or without.)

Week 28

Teach Your Child a Skill

One of the best ways to build self-esteem, courage, and your relationship with your child is by taking the time to teach her a skill—anything from practicing with her to improve a sports skill to introducing a brand new skill such as cooking a soufflé. Make sure that your child is interested in learning the skill and that it is age appropriate. Don't try to teach a toddler how to build an engine or a teen how to color within the lines. A good variation on this activity is to let your child teach *you* something, or to learn something together. Follow these tips and you'll find that the time you spend together will pay off in multiple ways.

1. Motivate. Encourage your child to want to learn the skill by being enthusiastic and explaining how it will serve him and/or the entire family.

2. Select a good time. Pick a time when neither you nor your child is rushed.

3. Break the skill down into baby steps. The encouragement of experiencing many small successes along the way is vital to your child's motivation to continue.

4. Demonstrate. Kids learn a lot by watching, so demonstrate each step. However, be careful NOT to say how easy it is. It may be easy for you, but that just makes your child feel like an idiot when he has trouble doing what you told him was easy.

5. Let your child try. Be ready to offer support and help if she needs it.

6. Encourage effort as well as results. Your words of encouragement ("attagirl, way to go, keep trying, nice one, now you're getting it, yes!") will make her feel good about herself, her progress, and you.

7. Work or play together. This not only reinforces the learning, but it's part of the enjoyment and the relationship building.

Work/play together • Encourage effort • Let your child try • Demonstrate • Break the skill down into baby steps • Select a good time • Motivate

Activity

Remember When... (and Now)

Think back to when you were a child and recall something that one of your parents, or even a grandparent, taught you to do.

What did you learn to do?

What did you like about the experience?

What did you dislike about it?

What will you do differently with your own child?

Now, take some time to teach your own child (or children) a skill, being sure to pay attention to the seven tips. Then answer these questions...

What did you teach your child?

What did you like about the experience?

What will you do differently next time?

Find Ways to Encourage

I have a confession to make. I've been beating around the bush. If you want to know the real secret to parenting, this is it: find ways to encourage your children. As child psychiatrist Rudolph Dreikurs once put it:

"Children need encouragement like plants need water."

In fact, encouragement is so important to a child that without it kids either shrink into nothing or resort to misbehavior in order to feel like something. Either way, it's not a pretty sight.

The word "encourage" itself means "to instill courage." And the word courage comes from the French word *coeur,* meaning "heart." When kids have courage they pursue their goals through positive behavior, are willing to risk failure, and keep trying. Without courage, kids become "dis-couraged," turn to negative behavior, or give up on themselves.

This is such an important topic that during the next four weeks I'll be presenting specific ways to encourage your child and to build self-esteem and confidence. We'll start this week with a simple yet powerful method of encouragement: Simply send this author $100 with a short note describing how much this book has already meant to you. This will encourage him greatly. Oh, all right...skip the $100 part and the note actually goes to your child and not me, but otherwise it's a great activity.

Encourage (en•kur•ij), verb: to instill courage

Activity

Letter of Encouragement

Putting it in writing is such a powerful force in our society that a written letter of encouragement will often carry much more weight than the mere words themselves. Write each of your children a short letter focusing on his strengths and areas of improvement. Then either mail the letter or put it someplace where each child will find it. And no e-mailing! They should have a hard copy to keep and reread whenever they want to. With very young children, you can read it to them. (If you have to read it to your ten-year-old, you might want to reread the last week's lesson on teaching skills.) Keep a few tips in mind as you write:

- **Focus on improvement, not perfection.**

- **Be sincere or they will see through you like a greedy relative at a funeral.**

- **Be specific about what you like and about the improvements.**

- **Include how the child's positive behavior has been helpful to others.**

Don't expect a big thank you from your child or for him to suddenly stop complaining when you send him to bed on time. Just know that underneath the surface your words will have an encouraging impact that will nourish his roots like fertilizer.

Hey, look Mom! No chart this week!

Week 30

Stimulate Independence

Another great child psychologist, Chaim Ginott, said "dependence breeds hostility." If you don't think so just ask King George III. He kept the American colonies dependent as long as he could and boy did they become hostile! On the other hand, Thomas Jefferson's mother read in a parenting book to "stimulate your child's independence" and the rest, as they say, is (American) history.

Parents who are overly *autocratic*, dictator-like, and act as if they are the rulers and their kids the peasant class often wind up with rebellious kids. However, parents who take a *permissive* approach to parenting, who act like doormats allowing their kids to walk all over them, often wind up with kids who are spoiled little socio-paths. The key to parenting in a democratic society is the concept of "freedom within limits." As kids get older and more responsible the *authoritative* parent gradually allows the child to make more and more of her own decisions. Stimulate your child's independence with these and other ideas:

- **Avoid pampering.** Teach them to do things for themselves as their age and ability allow. This includes self care (teeth brushing and shoe tying), family chores, getting themselves up in the morning, and in short, not doing for them on a regular basis what they can do for themselves.

- **Don't overprotect.** Part of our job as parents is to keep our kids from being run over by trucks and abducted by strangers. However, we can overdo it and stifle their independence. Talk with other parents about what is reasonably safe in your community and allow your child appropriate freedom. Also remember that our job does not include protecting our kids from the bumps, bruises, and even stitches of childhood, nor the hurt feelings. Such adversity can help a child develop the emotional muscle he will need to survive and thrive in life.

Activity

Pass the Buck

Think of something that you've been doing for your child that she could be doing for herself, then pass the responsibility on to her. Maybe it's a simple household chore like filling the dishwasher after dinner or installing a new roof. (That's to point out that you want to keep it appropriate for her age and ability.) This does not have to be a chore, either. If you have been picking up her clothes off the floor or getting her up for school, these would be good tasks to pass on. Once you have decided what to turn over to her, sit down and share the information in an encouraging way.

This means NOT: "I'm sick and tired of doing all the work around here so from now on you're going to have to load the dishwasher after dinner if you want any allowance."

This is more encouraging: "You know, I've been treating you like you were too delicate to help out around here, and I apologize. I know that you can do a lot more than I have given you credit for. Plus, to be honest, I could really use the help. What would you like to do to help out in the kitchen? For example, would you rather load the dishwasher after dinner or sweep up the kitchen? (Remember Week 4 about giving choices!) Either one would be a big help."

And of course, once they start helping (which may take a few reminders since this is a new habit) be sure to offer lots of encouragement.

What job will you pass on to your child?

What will you say to keep it encouraging?

How did it go?

Build On Strengths
with the BANK Method

A psychology class decided to do an experiment…on their professor. He had been lecturing on the power of positive reinforcement and they wanted to show him how well they had learned the lesson by getting him to lecture from the side of the room opposite from where he normally stood. So every time the professor moved in the direction they wanted him to, the class encouraged him by looking attentive, taking notes, and answering his questions. But when he drifted back to his usual position, they looked disinterested, yawned, and failed to respond. By the end of the class, he had moved all the way to the other side of the room.

Encouragement is powerful stuff. When we pay attention and acknowledge our kids' strengths and assets they usually continue to improve in these areas. But when we ignore them these strengths often diminish. The BANK method can help you use the power of encouragement to build your child's strengths— whether it is a sports skill, academic skill, or character trait:

B...**Baby steps.** Break the skill or trait down into small steps.

A...**Acknowledge** what your child already does well. Be sure to point out your child's current strengths on the road from A to Z.

N...**Nudge** him to take the next step. Change can be challenging, sometimes even scary. Be careful though, and don't push too fast or too hard. Sometimes progress is about two steps forward and one step back.

K...**Keep encouraging.** Give a lot of "good job" and "attaboy" as he continues to move in the positive direction. Your encouragement and his success will keep motivation high until the goal is finally reached.

Baby Steps • Acknowledge • Nudge • Keep Encouraging

BANK on it!

Think of a skill or character trait that you want to work with your child to improve. Use the following chart to help you use the BANK method to accomplish this goal. This may be something that you choose to discuss with your child, or like the psychology class, you can take a more subtle approach and just use your encouraging attention to bring about results over time.

What skill or trait do you want to encourage?

What are some Baby steps to take?
1.
2.
3.
4.
5.

What will you Acknowledge to your child that she is already doing well?

How can you Nudge your child to take the next step?

List ways that you can Keep encouraging progress as it occurs:

Week 32

Show Confidence

A mother eagle was flying south for the winter when an ice storm forced her to seek shelter in the chicken coop of a nearby farm. While waiting out the weather she laid an egg, which she eventually left behind as she continued on her way to meet friends in South Beach. (This is not the part of the story I want you to emulate.) The egg was sat upon by chickens, eventually hatched, and the baby eagle was raised as one of the chickens. This eagle who now thought he was a chicken did what chickens did: scratched the earth for bugs, ran scared of bigger animals, and never flew more than a few feet. One day the eagle was out in the farmyard with a chicken when a beautiful bird flew overhead. "What is that?" asked the eagle. "Oh, that is an eagle," replied the chicken. "He's king of the sky, but we are just lowly chickens down here on earth." And with that, the eagle who thought he was a chicken, went back to living out the rest of his life as a chicken.

My question to you is what are you raising—an eagle or a chicken?

For the nature buffs out there, you're right. Eagles don't migrate. But I'm sure you'll grant me some poetic license to make a point, right?

Help Your Child SOAR!

There are many ways for you to show confidence in your child, confidence that will not just improve his behavior, but will also boost his self-esteem and courage. For example:

- **Give responsibility.** Letting your child know that "I think you can handle this" is a big deal to many kids, whether it is caring for a pet or getting himself up in the morning. Of course, keep your expectations in line with his age and level of ability. Then use the BANK method (Week 31) and tips for teaching skills (Week 28) to set him up for success.
- **Ask your child's opinions and advice.** When you ask your child her opinion or advice it shows that you have confidence in her thinking.
- **Avoid the temptation to take over.** Instead of taking over a task from a child who is struggling, show confidence that he can work through the problem and succeed. You can offer help and support while showing confidence in his ability to stick with it and eventually succeed.

Look for opportunities this week to show confidence in your child. Then write down what you did and how your child responded.

How did you show confidence?	How did your child respond?	What will you do differently next time?

Week 33

Value Your Child "As Is"

The first book that I ever wrote was a satire on perfectionism called *So, Why Aren't You Perfect Yet?* In it I had the pleasure of poking fun at the tendency in our culture to pursue "more and more" and "better and better" in a vain attempt to finally be good enough. This feeling that "I will finally be good enough when…" is bad enough for adults, but the real tragedy is that we also pass it along to our kids.

Parents who constantly raise the bar on their children and act as if nothing is quite enough undermine their children's self-esteem in ways that may not show up for years. Many kids raised with overly high expectations do in fact succeed. However, they pay a terrible price, never really enjoying their victories for fear of the next challenge to their worthiness, and never quite feeling that elusive ideal of self-satisfaction.

One the other hand, kids who are loved unconditionally by their parents have a real leg up in the self-esteem category. They learn that win, lose, or draw they are loved and are worthwhile human beings. (Reminds me of the Tim Wakefield story I mentioned in Week 17.) They still strive to achieve, but they don't judge their lives solely on the basis of their achievements. They understand that happiness also comes from the quality of their relationships with others, and that right now, just as they are, they are already good enough.

Practice What I Preach

My wife will tell you that although I wrote the book on perfection, I am not perfect at this stuff either. We are all part of this achievement-oriented society and we all fail at times to value our children just as they are. Focus this week on three methods of doing this, and I'll do the same in my home. And who knows, maybe one of us will become perfect at it. (Whoops, I already lost.)

- **Separate worth from accomplishments.** Let your kids know that you love them for themselves, and not for what they achieve. Stress the joy of learning, and not just the grades; stress the joy of playing the game, and not just winning.

- **Separate worth from misbehavior.** There are no bad kids, only bad behavior. Never call kids names, even positive names (because she can figure out that if she fails to live up to the positive, then you will believe she has become the negative.)

- **Appreciate your child's uniqueness.** Every child has unique qualities that are lovable. It may be a smile, a laugh, the way she lights up when she sees you, or any of a million things that makes her special. Let your child know that you notice and appreciate these things.

How did you...

    separate worth from accomplishments?

    separate worth from misbehavior?

    appreciate your child's uniqueness?

Week 34

Act As a Filter for Your Child

Don't you just love a good filter? You probably haven't thought about it much, but filters are designed to do a wonderful thing: keep the dirt and other bad stuff out of a system. Because once bad stuff gets in there it circulates, contaminating and generally yucking up the entire works. Kids are systems, too, made up of thoughts, values, attitudes, feelings, and behavior. And one of our jobs as parents is to keep out as much bad stuff as we can. In our society this is pretty much an impossible task, so don't look for perfection. Instead, look to reduce the amount of dirt and other value-tainting stuff that gets to your kids. Then trust your other parenting skills to help your child be strong enough to withstand what gets by you. Here are some tips to help you become a positive filter in your child's life:

- **Monitor their viewing habits.** Use rating codes, computer screening devices, and your own values to determine what is okay and what is not okay for your kids to view.

- **And don't forget their music.** Don't worry about the notes, every generation manages to find sounds that their parents find offensive. That's okay. What's not okay is overly sexual, violent lyrics.

- **You can't pick their friends, but you can influence their choices.** It is usually unwise to forbid your child to see a friend. (Although if your child's friends are lawbreakers, go for it!) Otherwise, be more subtle.

- **Filter IN positive influences.** The more sources of healthy information and positive values that your child is exposed to, the better. Youth groups, spiritual education, sports, positive adults, and family members and friends all offer great ways to get more of the good stuff into the system.

Media Awareness Week

You're going to hate me for this, but I want you to spend 2-3 hours this week watching what your child watches and listening to what he listens to. Do not judge or criticize him for it, just raise your own awareness level. Later, discuss your views with him and come up with an agreement for what is okay and not okay to ingest. And do not fall victim to the old saw about what Billy is allowed to watch. The answer to that is, *"You're not Billy and I'm not Billy's mother. Now let's discuss how we are going to do it in our family."*

	Television	Movies	Internet	Music
Describe what you saw/heard.				
Was it mostly good stuff or bad stuff in your value system? How? Why?				
How will you filter it out if necessary?				

Character Talk: Alcohol and Other Drugs

If your child is under the age of seven, you can skip this one and go have yourself a stiff drink. While you are having that drink, you might consider the fact that about 90% of kids today experiment with alcohol and other drugs. A lot of these kids eventually get addicted, killed, or just into a lot of trouble from this "pursuit of happiness." Most parents who try to keep their kids away from these influences (remember the "filter" role we talked about last week) do so by threatening massive amounts of punishments if their kids become users or get caught experimenting. The trouble with this approach is that it wears off at about age 18 when the child leaves home. That's one reason we see so many 18- to 24-year-olds going wild.

A better approach is to use some discipline coupled with some persuasive talking. We call these short talks "character talks" because they are designed to build good character and not just good behavior. Here are some tips for having an effective character talk about alcohol and other drugs, and other topics as well:

- **Plan how you will introduce the topic.**
- **Write down key points you want to cover.**
- **Ask your child open-ended questions to stimulate discussion.**
- **Listen with empathy (no put downs!) as you discuss the topic together.**
- **Share your own values persuasively.**
- **Use support materials.**
- **Encourage your child's positive comments.**

Activity

Talk and/or Cut

Do your preparation and then have a short (15-20 minutes) character talk about alcohol and other drugs. Don't feel like you need to cover everything in one talk. The idea is to have many short talks instead of one long one.

Some families, especially with younger children, are more hands-on than verbal. If this is the case in your family, or if you want to combine two good activities, you can make a collage out of pictures and words from old magazines that present your family's values regarding alcohol and other drugs. This has the added benefit of creating a visual reminder of the talk that you can frame and put up in your home to remind everyone what you believe.

Write down a few key points you want to be sure to make:

_____

_____

After the talk...
How did it go? How did your child respond?

_____

What did you like about how you led the talk?

_____

What will you do differently next time?

_____

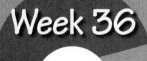

Week 36

Your Family's History

When my grandfather came to America he, like a lot of immigrants, did not speak much English. The good news is that he had relatives here who did. The challenge was to get from New York, where he was, to Augusta, GA, where they was (English is still a tricky language for his descendents). Fortunately for him he had two things in his favor: a train ticket and a red trunk. So, he got on the train and every time the train stopped at a station, my grandfather got off to see if the red trunk had been put off yet. When it finally did, he knew he must be in Augusta.

That's the story my father told me and I've passed down to my children. Telling and retelling the stories of your family's history, especially how you came to this country, gives your children a sense of roots—that they come from something grounded in history, that they aren't alone, because they have ancestors. All families have stories of courage and determination that can give your children additional role models for building their own strengths. Of course, we also have our horse thieves and renegades, but if you won't tell about these colorful folk, I won't tell either.

Activity

Tell Me a Story

Does your family have a special story that has been passed down from generation to generation? If not, this is as good a time as any to start one. Talk to your parents, grandparents, or any other living relative (dead won't work unless you are really good at séances) and find out how you came to this country and any interesting stories that capture some of the courage, ingenuity, or other attributes you might want to pass on. Then find a quiet time to tell these stories to your children. You can make it more interesting by asking questions afterwards. For example:

- What was your favorite part of the story?

- What is something special about this person?

- What do you admire about him or her?

- How can we show some of these same qualities in our lives?

- What if they made this into a major motion picture, who would you like to star in it?
  Would we get a percentage of the profits? Why not? Can you say, "creative accounting?"

What is the story? (Write it down so you will always remember it.)

_____

_____

_____

_____

_____

Week 37

Your Child's Education: Get Involved!

Here's an easy multiple choice question: Which of the following has been shown in over 200 studies to be the best predictor of a child's success in school?

- a) Quality of the teachers
- b) Quality of the school
- c) Child's intelligence
- d) Family's income
- e) Parent involvement

If you answered anything but "e" you either failed to read the title of this week's chapter or you must have thought this was a trick question. In any event, the fact is that your child needs your involvement to do her best and get the most out of her education. But what does parent involvement really mean? Glad you asked. Among other things it means:

- Developing a structured, but not rigid, home environment that promotes learning.
- Having high, but realistic, expectations for your child's success.
- Encouraging problem solving, curiosity, and independent thinking in your children.
- Encouraging positive behavior.
- Modeling lifelong learning.
- Building positive parent-child relationships.
- Supporting the discipline policy of the school.
- Understanding your child's learning styles.
- Encouraging language development through reading, talking, and listening.
- Making learning a part of everyday life.
- Becoming a positive coach when helping your child with schoolwork.

Activity

The Great Child School Interview

To see how much you know about your child's school life (which if you are like most parents is less than you might think) answer the following questions. Then interview your child and compare your answers with your child's.

	Your answers	Your child's answers
Who is your child's favorite teacher of all time?		
What is your child's favorite subject?		
What subject does your child do best in?		
Where does your child prefer to do her homework?		
Who is your child's best friend at school?		
What is one of your child's favorite books of all time?		
If your child had to choose a career right now, what would he choose?		

Your Child's Learning Style

Learning does not occur the same way for everyone. Some kids can lie on their bed with their feet high against the wall and absorb world history like sponges. Other kids like to camp out at the kitchen table close to the hum of daily life while they crunch the numbers of their math homework. Some like music in the background while others would be driven insane with music in the background. Some kids get it when they see it. Others do better when they hear it explained to them. Still others like to use their hands and learn best by doing. These differences in how kids learn are often referred to as learning styles. And parents do well to respect these differences, and even encourage them, within reason. What is within reason? For starters, no watching TV while doing homework and no hard rock music or hip hop in the background either. These things actually interfere with learning as anyone over the age of 30 has long suspected.

Educators have also noticed that intelligence comes in different flavors. Some kids have high verbal intelligence and are good with words— reading and writing them like crazy. Others have a mathematical or logical intelligence and are good at math and problem solving. Other forms of intelligence include musical, spatial, kinesthetic (that's body movement, like dance or sports), interpersonal ("people people"), and intrapersonal (intuitive people who like to march to their own drummer). Parents can encourage and build on their children's strengths, while helping them work to improve areas of deficit. Be particularly sensitive to the child whose talents differ from your own. You may be a gifted writer, but your child may be better at music. You can acknowledge and encourage his music, while helping him learn to improve his writing.

Identifying Talents

Think about the seven types of intelligence for yourself and your children. Then fill in the chart with a number from 1 (weakest) to 10 (strongest). Look at where you and your children are similar and different. Then sometime this week find something encouraging to say to your child about one of her strengths.

Type of Intelligence	You	Child #1	Child #2	Child #3	Child #4
Verbal					
Mathematical					
Musical					
Spatial (visual)					
Kinesthetic (physical)					
Interpersonal					
Intrapersonal					

Positive Encouragements:

Child #1
....

Child #2
....

Child #3
....

Child #4

The Importance of Structure

Structure is to a child what structure is to the house in which the child lives. It's the framework on which everything else hangs. When it's strong and well planned, everything else holds up pretty well. But when structures go awry you may as well live in a grass hut during tornado season, because things are going to start flying apart. That convoluted analogy aside, here's what I'm talking about: time, space, and behavior.

Time structures: Having routines for regularly occurring activities gives kids anchors that provide security and develop good habits. As kids get older you can shorten these routines and leave more to the child to decide. Some of the best include bedtime and morning routines, weekend bedtimes (not "whenever I get tired"), and calendars for activities, carpools etc.

Space structures: Help your child organize his room, take a picture of it, and post it in his room so he will remember what it looks like in case he never sees it like this again. Learning to keep things organized and reasonably neat is a good skill to develop while you are young. Tackle his closet together on some rainy Saturday afternoon. Establish an "everything in its place" philosophy.

Behavior structures (rules and guidelines): Establishing how things are done in your family helps your child know what's expected and how to meet those expectations. For example: rules for mealtime, safety rules, health rules.

Final note: You can be too structured and you can be too unstructured. The idea is moderation and common sense.

Activity

Establish a Routine

Pick an area such as bedtime in which you would like to establish a more consistent routine. (On the other hand, if you are already overly structured, pick a routine that has become burdensome and ease up on it.) Use the chart below to fill in the various aspects of the routine and to evaluate how it is working. Then modify it as your experience suggests.

Steps of routine	How did it go?	Do you need to modify? If so, how?

Week 40

Structure Homework Time

Given a choice, if your child would rather do homework than play or goof off, then there is something seriously wrong and you should seek immediate professional help. Let's face it, most kids believe that homework was invented by a monster and that it's perpetuated by the monster's unholy brood. Or perhaps it is the human race's punishment for Adam and Eve eating the fruit of knowledge in the Garden of Eden.

Anyway, homework is likely to be around for at least as long as it takes educators to figure out how to otherwise transfer knowledge into their heads. So, it behooves parents to set up an effective homework structure in their families. Some tips:

- **Help your child pick a quiet work area** with a good reading light and writing surface. Respect his learning style, but make sure the area is reasonably quiet.

- **Agree on a regular time for studying.** Some kids like to get to it right after school while others have activities or just want a break. After dinner is another good time. Five minutes before bedtime doesn't cut it very well.

- **Help your child develop a homework "to do" list.** It's good to learn young not to trust your memory when you have a perfectly good pen and paper to do the remembering for you (or even a PDA these days).

- **Be available to offer help, but don't take over.** And don't make a habit of doing their homework with or for them. If you are doing their homework for them then I hope you are prepared to go on to college with them also. As your child gets older, the best help you can offer may only be to help them figure out who to call to get some real help (and this way you don't have to admit it's over your head).

Activity

Homework Evaluation Project for Parents

Your homework for this week… wait a minute. Notice how I've been using the term "activity" instead of "homework" throughout this book. That's because adults don't like doing homework either. We didn't like it as kids, and we sure don't want to put up with it as adults. Now, activities…that's a different story. So, your "home activity" for this week is to evaluate your child's homework routine and the role you are playing. Then modify it with your child's input and cooperation as necessary. And if the dog eats your activity, you still get a zero. *Caution: If your child already has a system that works well, do not mess with it.*

Does your child have a regular homework time?

Does he have a good place to study?

Is there adequate lighting and a good writing surface?

Does your child make and use a "to do" list?

Are you available to help if needed?

Do you help too much?

Do you show an interest in his work?

Work with Your Child's Teacher

Let's pretend you are a teacher. A parent you've never met comes to you with a problem with her child. You can tell from her body language and tone of voice that she is not your best friend. In fact, as she begins to talk you get the unpleasant feeling that she thinks that *you* are the problem. Being a normal human being, you start to get defensive as your mind races towards self-protection. The parent attacks. You defend. Maybe it's subtle or maybe it's blatant, but the result is the same. Nobody is really focusing on how to help the child, and the child suffers.

Next, a parent who volunteers to help with activities, always seems to have an encouraging word for you, and seems to genuinely appreciate your contribution to her child's education comes to see you with a problem. She uses Doc Pop's handy-dandy "cooperative problem solving model." Together you find a solution for your student and feel better about yourselves in the process.

Don't you wish that you had this wonderful cooperative problem solving model? Wish no more:

1. Set up a meeting with the teacher.
2. Focus on your common goal: to help your child succeed.
3. Write down your concerns before you get to the meeting.
4. Ask the teacher how she sees the problem.
5. Find the common ground.
6. Bring a solution, not just a problem.
7. Agree on a course of action.
8. Agree on how you will follow up.
9. Monitor progress.
10. Evaluate the situation at a follow-up meeting.

Activity

Encourage Your Child's Teacher

Everybody needs encouragement and teachers are part of everybody. In fact, they could probably use a little extra encouragement since all kids aren't as wonderful as yours and mine. There are also benefits involved in encouraging your child's teacher.

First, when a teacher feels supported by her students' parents she feels better about herself, her job, and her mission to help educate students. This makes her a better teacher for your kids. Second, people tend to feel better about people who make them feel better about themselves. Encouragement does that. When you establish a positive relationship with your child's teacher, she is naturally going to be a little more sensitive to your child's needs.

This week take a moment to encourage your child's teacher. You can drop by in person or you can drop her a note. Most schools have e-mail now and that makes a very convenient way to connect. For example:

> Dear Mrs. Hickman,
> I just wanted to take a moment to thank you for all the help that you have given Michael this year. He has been learning so much, and I know how much time and effort you have put into the class. Maybe more important, you have such a special way of nurturing the kids that I'm sure they will all not only be better students, but better people, for having had you as their teacher this year.
> Sincerely,
> Mrs. Popkin

Well, maybe you aren't as crazy about your child's teacher as I was about Mrs. Hickman, my second grade teacher. But you can still find positive things to write or say. Just be truthful, be specific, and stay positive.

Support Your School's Discipline Efforts

There is a scene in my video-based parent involvement program, *Parents on Board,* in which a mother gets a phone call one evening from her son's teacher. As she listens and responds to the teacher, her son grows visibly less comfortable. When she finishes her conversation she turns to her son and sits him down for a one-on-one. "What were you thinking, talking to your teacher that way?" she admonishes him. They talk about the importance of respect and then a little later she explains, "You have to understand that when you get in trouble at school you are also in trouble at home." She follows this up with the logical consequence of having to write a letter of apology to his teacher. She says that she is letting it go at that, because this is the first time she has heard of him talking disrespectfully to a teacher, but that if it happens again, the consequences will be more stringent.

It is important for parents to get to know and support their school's discipline plan. Many schools have one in writing these days, so ask for it. If you have a problem with part of the plan, make an appointment to talk with the principal, but do not criticize the plan in front of your kids. This will just undermine the school's efforts and perhaps lead your children to think that they can ignore the rules. A lot of teaching time is wasted on discipline these days, time that could be saved if parents supported the school's policies like the mother in the video scene did. When kids learn that parents and the school are on the same side, they are less likely to test the rules to see what they can get away with. This ends up being better for everybody, especially the child.

Got a Plan? Get a Plan! Review the Plan.

This week I want you to get a copy of your school's discipline plan and review it with your child. If the school asks why you want it, tell them it's for your attorney. (Just kidding, although it is tempting.) Actually, tell them that you want to go over the plan with your child so he'll know what's expected and so you can support the plan. When you talk with your child or children about the plan, make it a discussion and not a lecture. Ask them what they think about various aspects of the plan, and explain why the school has likely included each part. Make it clear that your kids do not have to agree with everything in the plan, but they are expected to abide by everything in it.

What did you learn from reviewing the plan?

_____

_____

_____

How did your child respond to going over the plan together?

_____

_____

_____

What aspects of the plan will you want to keep in mind and perhaps review with your child again later?

_____

_____

_____

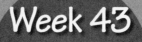

Week 43

Coaching Your Child to be an Effective Learner

The world of the 21st century in which your child will live and work will be less about reciting facts and more about thinking, communicating, problem-solving, cooperating in teams, and applying concepts in meaningful ways. Of course information will still be important, but with computers and search engines able to sift through vast amounts of information at incredible speeds, the human's job will be to use that information creatively, think critically, and stay motivated. Schools are adapting to these changes, and parents can help by coaching their kids along these lines. Although your job is not to teach, you can help your children in school through positive coaching. Keep these seven principles in mind:

1. Be available. Don't do it for them, but offer support and guidance if needed.

2. Offer support, not criticism. Find something positive to say before pointing out errors. Never, ever, ever attack the child's personality.

3. Focus on effort instead of grades. The grades will come.

4. You don't have to be an expert to help. Don't be afraid to say, "I don't know."

5. Don't expect perfection. Academic success is neither synonymous with happiness nor is it the measure of a good life. So, keep it light and fun.

6. Turn the thinking over to the child. Don't fall into the trap of doing the work for your child. Let her struggle a little bit for the answer and enjoy the success of getting it herself.

7. Enjoy! Make learning enjoyable by smiling, laughing, and basking in each other's company.

Activity

Coach the Kid!

Look for an opportunity this week to coach your child with a project, homework assignment, or some other academic endeavor. Review the seven steps before you do, and then fill out the chart to evaluate how you did. Finally, consider saying a little prayer of thanks that you finished school before it got so complicated!

Did you remember to...	How did it go?	What would you do differently next time?
Be Available		
Offer support, not criticism		
Focus on effort		
Remember you don't have to be an expert		
Not expect perfection		
Turn the thinking over to your child		
Enjoy!		

Week 44

Read with Your Child

The best thing that you can ever do for your child to help him academically is to give him some really smart genes. Too late? Okay, the next best thing is to read to him every day. Reading is the key to learning almost anything, and our schools are heavily geared to rewarding good readers. Start reading to your child as soon as his eyes can focus on the pictures—earlier if you like. As kids get older, they can read to you or you can pick books that are too advanced for them and read them to your child. A good goal is to read together twenty minutes daily.

Be sure to remember to use your coaching skills to keep the experience positive. Then to really enhance the experience, work in some of the following types of questions to teach thinking skills:

- Encourage observation by asking who, what, where, and when questions during the story or after the end of a short story.

- Encourage your child to think ahead by asking her to predict what she thinks might happen next.

- Encourage language skills by asking the meaning of unusual words and discussing them together. Try looking up words in the dictionary together.

- Reinforce memory by asking the child what happened in the last segment you read together.

- Encourage analytical thinking by asking him why he thinks the author had the character do what he did.

- Encourage self-esteem and a love for learning by making positive comments when your child answers these questions.

Reading Aloud Plus

If you do not read to your child on a regular basis, and your child is not a teenager yet, pick a book that you think she would like and begin today. If your child is a teenager, pick a play or movie script and read that together, each taking various parts. (This can be a lot of fun if you get into the spirit of it.) Then, regardless of whether you are already reading together or just beginning, use some of the "questions to teach thinking skills" previously mentioned to enhance the experience. Keep it fun and enjoyable and you'll find that you don't need a $100 million film budget to make a book come to life.

What did you read?

What questions did you ask?

How did it go?

What will you do differently next time?

Week 45

Monitor Screen Time

We've had a really good policy in our family throughout our children's lives: no TV on school nights and limited TV on weekends. The amount of time this has saved our family is immeasurable. Well, actually it is measurable. Let's see, if the average child watches four hours of TV a day, by my estimation we will have saved about 400 days for each child over the course of their school careers! That's over a full year each! Imagine how much time they have had for more worthwhile endeavors. No wonder they're perfect! (OK... but you get the idea.)

There was one little fly in our ointment. One weekend I discovered that after I had chased my son off the television he would simply go to the computer for hours. Soon we realized that we had to limit not just TV, but all screen time. It seems that whatever flickers light attracts these kids like flames attract moths. There are two problems with this: 1) too much screen time interferes with more beneficial activities; 2) there are some real risks out there on the Internet. Every day there are adult predators scanning the Internet chat rooms for kids to seduce into harmful relationships. These relationships have tragic consequences. A few guidelines can help:

1. No talking to strangers online.
2. Tell your child to never ever give out his full name, phone number, or address online, or the name of his school.
3. The computer stays in a public area where parents can peek in to see that the child is abiding by the guidelines.
4. Agree to a limit on television and other screen activities.
5. Check all video games and movies for violence and sexual content. Decide what you are comfortable with. Use the labeling system on movies for hints.

Activity

Screen Time Meeting

Have a meeting with your kids to discuss issues of screen time. Specifically discuss:

1. How much time is okay to watch for school nights and weekends?
2. What limits on content will each child adhere to—based on age?
3. What dangers exist on the Internet and what rules will you establish together to keep everyone safe?

As with all meetings that involve guidelines, make sure that you:

- Are caring and not judgmental. If you get overly moralistic or judgmental you will turn them off and create problems. Make sure they know how much you love them and want them to stay safe and develop into successful people.
- Ask questions and discuss. Don't lecture.
- Write down all agreements and post them if necessary.
- Encourage your children's good ideas and positive values. (*"Good idea." "I like that." "That makes sense." "That's very mature of you."*)

Afterward, review with following questions:

How did the meeting go?

What agreements did you make?

1.
2.
3
4.

What will you do differently next time?

Week 46

SQ3R Technique for Successful Studying

Sometimes the stress to always do one's best is better balanced with some enjoyment of learning and relaxation in life. Having said that, we both know that you want your child to have good options for college, and that means good grades, and that means doing well on tests. Some kids know how to study and do very well on their own. If you have such a child proceed with caution. You don't want to mess up a good thing.

On the other hand, most kids can use some help, and one excellent technique for studying is called the "SQ3R" technique, because it was invented by a scientist of the same name: Professor Herr Docktor SQ3R. (How he got to use a 3 in his name is a great mystery.) Actually, SQ3R stands for:

Survey: Look over the entire assignment or chapter by first reading only title, subheadings and captions.

Question: Ask questions about the material. What's the purpose of this material? How does it fit with what we are studying? Try to guess at what the headings suggest the material will teach.

Read: Read the material carefully, making notes.

Recite: Without looking back at the material, teach your child to answer questions about the material. What are the main ideas? What are the important facts and details? What will the teacher likely ask about on a test?

Review: Have your child go back over the material after some time has passed. Have her make study guides of the important information and review until she knows it well.

Activity

Give SQ3R a Try

I'll admit that the SQ3R technique will probably sound pretty lame to your kids, and maybe to you as well. But a surprisingly large number of people have found that it really does help to improve learning and test scores. Plus, Dr. SQ3R's aging mother depends on the meager royalties generated every time a student uses this technique to fund her Bingo habit, so be a sport and get your child to give it a try. Work together at first, but be careful and don't take over. Stay encouraging and make lots of positive comments about your child's efforts. Later talk about the results together and see if it is a technique that your child wants to keep using.

SQ3R Steps	How did it go?
Survey	
Question	
Read	
Recite	
Review	

What were the results?

_____

Will your child use this technique again?

_____

Did you send Mrs. SQ3R her Bingo money?

_____

Week 47

Improving Language Skills

Let's face facts. In our culture it pays to be well spoken. People with better language skills, both verbal and written, are not just better communicators, they are also perceived as being more intelligent and capable as well. Often they actually are! Here are some tips for enhancing those skills in your child:

• **First, turn off the TV and computer games.** As I've said before, TV in moderation, especially good TV, is okay and even worthwhile. So are some computer/video games. However, talking together is a much better way to improve language skills, and not much talking occurs when the TV is blaring or the video game zapping.

• **Take time to talk with your child,** one to one and as a family. Family conversation can do more to build your child's mind and language skills than all the so-called educational games and toys you'll ever buy. Take advantage of dinner time, driving time, and other opportunities to talk together.

• **Play word games together.** Make up rhymes, reverse letters, use Pig Latin, play hangman and find other language games in books to help strengthen language skills while still having fun.

• **Choose books to read aloud** to your child that have good language.

• **Gently correct verbal errors** by suggesting the correct form. For example, *"He wented to the movies." "Yes, he went to the movies."*

• **Develop vocabulary** by looking up words that your child comes across that she doesn't know and then making index cards with the definitions. Then practice these words together. One guy started doing this in graduate school and raised his verbal GRE (a standardized test) score 100 points.

Activity

Mental Movie

Any of the previous tips would make a good activity, and I encourage you to explore as many as are reasonable for you and your child. In addition, try this "mental movie" activity to encourage accurate understanding and memory for what is read. To do this, read a story without pictures to your child (or don't show your child the pictures, if there are any until afterward). Then ask your child to close his eyes and imagine what something in the story looks like. It could be a monster, any character, or even a setting. Ask questions to help, like, "What color is your monster? Tell me more about what he looks like." Encourage your child by commenting on descriptive imagery and detail. *"I really like the way you put sharp teeth on the monster and had blood and guts dripping out of his mouth. That was a nice touch. I think I'll go throw up now."*

What book did you read?

How did your child describe the character or object?

How did you encourage him?

What will you do differently next time?

Week 48

Some Spelling Tips

Okay, time for true confessions: I'm not a very good speller. Fortunately spelling is not linked to intelligence. Comedian Brian Reagan has a hysterical bit he does about his encounter with the rules of spelling as a child. "Brian," asks his teacher, "What is the 'i' before 'e' rule?" "Uh...i before e." "Yes, Brian, but when does 'i' come before 'e'?" "Um...always?" "No, Brian. 'I' before 'e' except after 'c' and when sounding like 'a' as in 'neighbor' and 'weigh' and on Sundays and leap years and all throughout May, and you'll always be wrong no matter what you say!" (For some fun family bonding time, go get one of Brian's CDs and listen to it as a family.)

Like most things, spelling can be improved. I realize that with the spell checker on computers these days spelling skills aren't as important as they used to be. But spell check won't catch everything and it's not always available. So, here are a few tips for improving spelling:

- **Go over the rules of spelling.** In spite of Brian Reagan's humor, rules for spelling do help. Get a book on the subject and go over them with your child as necessary.

- **Memorize problem words.** We all have words that give us spelling migraines. The best approach is to notice which these are and then just memorize them. You can sometimes teach your child a memory gimmick to help. For example, for *desert/dessert*: dessert has two "s's" because it tastes so good you always want more.

- **Practice clapping syllables.** By clapping together with your child each syllable in a word, you can help her hear the sounds more clearly (unless you're clapping really loud) and improve spelling.

- **Use a multisensory approach:** "AKTV." (Just keep reading...)

The AKTV Technique

This multisensory approach to spelling involves four components: **A**uditory (sound), **K**inesthetic (movement), **T**actile (feel) and **V**isual (sight). Try it with your child on a difficult word to spell. For example: S-Y-L-L-A-B-L-E as in, "Pronounce each syllable for the word clearly and it will be easier to spell the word."

1. Have your child write down the word "syllable" (or another word) on a piece of paper. Then talk together about the letter patterns and sounds it contains. For example:

   - Three syllables, syl - la - ble, each containing an "l."

   - The middle syllable, "la," is a word in itself (the sixth note of the scale).

   - The "y" has a short "i" sound.

   - "ble" is a common word ending.

2. Trace the word with a finger while saying it aloud.

3. Next, have your child practice tracing the word with his finger on a rough surface such as a rug with his eyes closed. Have him say the word out loud as he is writing it. A variation is to have him write each syllable in a different color.

4. Finally, have him say the word out loud while writing it on paper. Check the spelling. Then cover the word up, say and write it again, and then once more.

If, after all this, he is still having trouble spelling "syllable," you might want to take a few minutes and write a thank you note to the programmer who invented spell check.

Make Math and Science Everyday Play

I know that this sounds like a stretch, but kids, especially young kids, are pretty naïve and have yet to discover that math and science are terrible things invented to make children and teens feel inferior. Though this statement is meant to be humorous, the sad truth is that many parents approach these important subjects as if they were just that. In fact, math and science have become so important in the 21st century that Harvard University recently revised its undergraduate curriculum to include more of them. They understood, as many forward-thinking schools and parents understand, that we live in an age of incredible advancements in science, and to understand these, let alone have a career in them, requires a good foundation in math and science. In addition, kids who learn to do well in these subjects are improving their ability to solve problems and reason effectively in the process, and these skills are vital to any 21st century career.

First, you can help your child by encouraging her in these subjects, always talking with a positive attitude and showing confidence in her ability to succeed. Then consider some of the following activities to make math and science relevant by using them in everyday life.

Activity

Math and Science In Action

Choose at least three of the following to try this week, keeping in mind your child's age and level of ability. Then fill in the chart to keep a record and evaluate:

1 With young kids, play counting games with the sugar packets at the restaurant.

2 When driving your child to oboe lessons play an exciting game of twenty questions or "animal, vegetable, or mineral."

3 Cook together. You'd be surprised at all the math and science involved in using recipes. Plus, it's fun and you can eat the results.

4 Make sure kids over the age of seven have a regular weekly allowance. Then help them learn to calculate how to spend and save.

5 The next time you take a trip, have your child help you plot the route on a map and then follow it. If you go by car, teach her to calculate your gas mileage.

6 Play inventor by talking together about cool invention ideas. It isn't necessary to actually build a time machine, just talking about the possibilities can help build creativity and appreciation for math and science. If you do build one, give me a call.

Activity	How did it go?	What will you do differently next time?

Week 50

Family Meeting: Solve a Problem

Back in Week 3, I suggested that problems are opportunities for teaching our children problem-solving skills and qualities of character such as courage and perseverance. The same is true for families. Each family has a personality just as each member in the family does. When faced with a problem does your family resort to bickering and blaming, or does it get serious about solving the problem? My kids are probably sick of hearing me say "solve the problem," but I'd rather them overlearn the lesson than think that problems just magically go away or have them wait for Prince Charming to show up. (Besides, I'm not so sure that spoiled old Prince C was all that effective a problem solver anyway. I mean, didn't he just bend down and kiss the girl and she woke up? Sounds more like luck than problem solving to me.) Here's a good method for family problem solving that we teach in our Active Parenting program:

1. Identify the problem. "I'd like to talk about how we will divide up chores."

2. Share thoughts and feelings. This provides an opportunity for each person to be heard and have his thoughts and ideas count.

3. Brainstorm possible solutions and guidelines. All ideas should be appreciated, as an unrealistic idea may trigger another idea that is closer to a solution.

4. Choose a solution that everyone can live with. The idea is to reach consensus. The solution may not be anyone's first choice, but must be one that everyone can support. If a consensus can't be reached, hold a vote. (Parents, as leaders in the family, make decisions in the cases of health and safety.)

5. Follow-up later. This makes sure that agreements have been kept. If they haven't, then maybe it's time for another meeting.

Activity

Family Fun Time

As a problem to practice on, call a meeting of the entire family to choose a fun activity for the family to spend a day doing. In today's busy world, finding a good day is a problem in itself, so begin there. You may also want to put some budgetary limits on the choices, or else be willing to fly to the kids' favorite theme park for the day. Remember the five steps of Active Problem Solving, and then fill in the chart after you get back from Orlando.

Step	How did it go?	What will you do differently next time?
Identify the problem.		
Share thoughts and feelings.		
Brainstorm possible solutions.		
Choose a solution everyone can live with.		
Follow up later.		

Write Your Child a Love Poem

I have this terrific stepmother who came into our family after the untimely death of my mother when I was seventeen. Being the loving, supportive person that she is, we bonded very quickly over lots of late-night talks my senior year in high school. Then, when I went off to college the next fall, she gave me an unexpected present: a poem she had written just for me. Now, you have to understand that my stepmother is not a writer, so this was a stretch for her. And although it may not have won any poetry awards, I'd swear that it was the most beautiful thing ever written, and I still have the original copy to this day. Why? Because it was a poem from the heart, one that spoke of her love for the new son in her life (she already had three of her own!) and her confidence that my strengths would make college a good experience for me.

When my daughter turned sixteen, I wrote her a love poem. I called it "Megan at Sixteen" (brilliant, huh?) and focused on all of her lovely assets. The first stanza goes,

> *Strong and purposeful you stride toward the future*
> *Like an athlete prepared to vault over life's hurdles*
> *Turning obstacles into opportunities to give you lift and rise.*

Megan is a gymnast and a basketball player, and this verse alludes to her role as "athlete." The other verses capture other roles she plays and the strengths that she exemplifies. But when all is said and done, the poem ends with what is really important:

> *Loving and spiritual, your pure heart beats strong*
> *Like a daughter who is loved for who she is*
> *Much more than for all the wonderful things you do.*

Activity

Go Ahead...Write the Poem

If you have never written a poem, you are in for a real treat. It's a creative experience that produces some powerful, positive feelings whether you are a gifted writer or not. You can choose to use rhyme or free verse as you please. It can be long or short. The important thing is that it comes from your heart and focuses on the love you feel for your child. A few tips might help you get going:

- Add some things that are specific to your child, so the poem doesn't sound as if it came off a greeting card.

- Go back to the picture of your child in the front of this book and use it for inspiration.

- Remember that this is a love poem, so keep it 100% positive. No lines like, "In spite of the problems we sometimes have..."

- Don't refer to roses or violets. They've been done to death.

- If you get stuck, go read some poetry for more inspiration.

- If you get really stuck, think about hitting yourself in the head with a 2x4. (Don't actually do this; just think about it. I have it on authority that Shakespeare used to do this before he wrote his sonnets, so it must work.)

- Make a draft of the poem, wait a day, then rewrite it to make any changes that you would like before giving it to your child. Most poets find this helps them improve their writing.

Finally, stick a copy of your poem between these pages in this book so you will always have it as a part of this process. Also, if you would like to share it with me, send me a copy at docpop@activeparenting.com. I'd love to hear from you.

Week 52

Your Strengths as a Parent

Well, our year together is almost done. (Like I actually believe that you spent exactly one year working through this book, doing all the activities, and are finally at the end. HA! Fifty-two weeks, my eye. If you've read this far, I bet you did it in less than a month. Either that or you skipped to the end, in which case you are probably disappointed not to find out "who done it." In either case, you may need to go back and re-read some portions, slowing down to do the activities. But in case I'm wrong, here's to our last week together!)

All parents have strengths on which to build. I hope that this book has helped you to build some new strengths as well as reminded you of many strengths you already had. But because parents need encouragement, too, let's not leave it at that. Take a look at the list on the next page of some of the parenting areas we have covered, and write down at least one strength that you have in each. Then, remembering that your job as a parent is one of the most difficult and important jobs in the world, take a few minutes to feel good about what you are contributing to your children, your family, community, and society through your efforts.

Building On Your Strengths

Write down at least one strength you have in each parenting area in the space below.
(Look... *sniff, sniff*... your last table!)

	A Strength You Have...
Relationship building	
Encouragement	
Discipline	
Taking time	
School Involvement	
Communication	
Taking Care of Yourself	
Love	

Congratulations! Your kids are lucky to have you.

Resources

Healy, Jane M. *Your Child's Growing Mind: Brain Development and Learning from Birth to Adolescence.* 3rd. ed. New York: Random House, 2004.

Popkin, Michael H. *Active Parenting Now Parent's Guide.* Atlanta, GA: Active Parenting Publishers, 2001.

_____. *Active Parenting of Teens Parent's Guide.* Atlanta, GA: Active Parenting Publishers, 1998.

Popkin, Michael H., Youngs, Bettie B., and Healy, Jane M. *Parents On Board: Helping Your Child Succeed in School.* Atlanta, GA: Active Parenting Publishers, 2001.

Popkin, Michael H., and Spizman, Robyn Freedman. *Getting Through to Your Kids: Easy Conversations about Difficult Things.* New York City: The Berkeley Publishing Group, 2002.

Youngs, Bettie B. *Keeping Your Children Safe: A Parent's Guide to Physical, Emotional, Spiritual and Intellectual Wellness.* San Diego: Learning Tools, 1993.

If you enjoyed this book and would like to learn more, check out our website:
www.ActiveParenting.com/parents.htm

There you'll find lots great resources for parents just like you, including a list of Active Parenting classes in your area, and an opportunity to participate in a parenting group conducted entirely over the Internet, for all you really busy parents!